AS IT
HAPPENED

AS IT HAPPENED

BARBARA FRUM

McClelland and Stewart

ISBN: 0-7710-3195-5

The Canadian Publishers
McClelland and Stewart Limited
25 Hollinger Road, Toronto

Printed and bound in Canada
by John Deyell Company

To Murray, who never tires of carrying us all. To David, whose terse reviews ("blah," "unintelligible," "if it weren't Nader it would stink") helped determine the pieces included here. To Linda, who sacrificed the most, and to Matthew, who poured the grapefruit juice.

Contents

Introduction:
Inside *As It Happens*

People have been phoning *in* to radio programs since the early 1950s. Phoning *out* – that was the breakthrough. Fast and cheap—and for CBC, cheap is often the more inspiring quality — radio can go anywhere instantly if it goes by telephone. The Middle East situation seems confused? We'll get you the Premier of Lebanon and let you judge for yourself. You read that Bryce Mackasey is furious with the postal union? We'll phone the minister and let you hear just how furious. For $2,100 worth of dimes a week we dial the world – not only for the facts, but for the sound and temperature of what is happening.

As far as I can tell, the *As It Happens* idea was invented by a West German radio station. That station's mix of music and phone-out interviews so captivated the wife of a CBC executive assigned to Canadian Armed Forces Radio in Europe that she became a secret fan, spurning her husband's brand of broadcasting. Being a clever man, as well as a forgiving one, he brought the phone-radio idea back with him to Canada. After a couple of experimental efforts, that format evolved into *As It Happens*.

I came to host the program in 1971. For the preceding three years I had done a similar job on the supper-hour TV news in Toronto. I quit when yet another managerial shake-up and a lingering timidity following the War Measures Crisis combined to demand QUIET. When my new bosses interpreted that demand to mean "friendlier" interviews from me personally, I decided to return to freelance writing. For someone who thinks of interviewing as a game full of surprises, it sounded a little too managed for my taste.

The very week I left that television job I was advised to sit tight and wait for the fall radio season. The people at CBC radio were doing a housecleaning of their programming schedule, which the executives – a little pretentiously –

proclaimed their "Radio Revolution." Under any name, it couldn't have come at a better moment. Television was in the doldrums. People who wanted information and a national voice on Canadian and international affairs were ready to be lured back to radio. The show I was invited to host was deliberately designed to break all the old, safe CBC rules. The orders were: provide an iconoclastic, zippy, nightly information package. Speak to everybody, not just to the few who genuflect to the sound of a mid-Atlantic accent. I've been on the dialling end of a telephone ever since.

Now, five years and 10,000 interviews later, I am astonished that some people still imagine me arriving at the studio each evening five minutes before air time, picking up the phone, and ordering up a menu with the operator: "Tonight, operator, let's start things off with the Shah of Iran. I feel like a cabinet minister next – Lalonde if you can, but he's rarely willing. Joe Clark would be great to hear after that. This guy who says Christopher Columbus was really a Johnny-come-lately sounds worth four minutes. Then let's see who's around who's funny." I'm touched that, after all this time, there are still listeners like the twelve-year-old Ottawa girl who, hearing Alan Maitland announce that we'd be talking about the murder of the king of Saudi Arabia, yelled out, "Hey Mommy, come quick, Barbara's dialling the man who killed King Faisal." It doesn't quite work like that.

I don't dial my own numbers, and – dare I confess – I don't talk on a telephone. I speak into a microphone that is electronically (which to me means "magically") hooked into the telephone system. Our guests talk into their telephones and I hear them through the headset that I wear over my ears. The show is done live. But it's not done just in the hour and a half we're on the air. We have to start our daily chase at noon in order to accommodate the waking hours of the world.

As for that other flattering misconception, that every story we do is Barbara Frum's idea – perhaps if I explain my mental image of the program you'll understand why that's unreasonable as well. I see *As It Happens* as a ravenous monster who every night must be served up sixteen virgin story ideas or else he'll die of starvation. This monster manages to devour every idea I get, plus all the ideas that an Executive Producer and nine full-time story hunters can throw at him. Only in the exhilaration of having completed another show can we relax and forget for a moment the inexorable cycle: tomorrow our monster will wake up famished and we will have to hunt down sixteen more beauties to appease him.

That beast's heroic appetite requires that for seven hours a day I sit on a padded kitchen chair in my little studio cage asking questions. While I do that, our all-knowing commander, the Executive Producer, whips onward nine frantic story producers. On the telephones upstairs they hunt down their quarry around the world, then tear down to the studio to brief me quickly so that I can mediate between the story and the listener. Each story comes at me shepherded by one of those producers. They function as advocates of their particular idea, pleading for special consideration for the guest they've managed to land, jockeying for position on the program, and always tense because *they* know the problems and I don't.

Thanks to a nifty torture device called a "talk-back," however, they've got it arranged so I'll not be ignorant for long. Through the talk-back my producers can buzz right into my ear without disturbing the guest on the line. I seem to spend my days, as a result, in two simultaneous conversations. In one ear is my guest on the telephone; in the other, my nervous, helpful colleagues. "Beirut is calling me back in five minutes, Barbara." "I'll delay New Delhi, but that means you'd better wind this up right away. By the way, there's someone at the front desk who says you promised to see him about his high school project." "Sorry, Barbara, I have to get Allmand before he's called to the House." "Dave's writing his Intro for the Portugal piece now. Did the guy say the election is Saturday or Sunday?" "Okay, wind up, please, here comes Buenos Aires."

To cope, I have to pull down my internal windowshade. I stare at the ugly beige linoleum on the kitchen table that serves as my combination studio desk, lunch counter, and communications centre, while I rummage through my brain

– pulling, pulling, pulling. What does this idea remind me of? Didn't someone tell us just the opposite last week? What was it I promised myself that I'd remember the next time I was talking to Beirut? And all the time I'm jotting notes and messages to myself as I barrel ahead into the line of stacked-up interviews.

June Callwood once asked me on her television show what I did with my anger and my frustration and my moods while I do those sixteen interviews required each day. "I put them all in a little brown paper bag," I told her. "I leave the bag at the door when I arrive every morning and I pick it up again each night and take it home." Every job, I'm convinced, has one component that nobody dares tell you about when you're hired. It's always something you only discover once you're on the premises. In my case, what they didn't tell me about was the relentless pressure.

When I first joined *As It Happens* we did something called roller-coasting, which was even more backbreaking. The theory was that we could keep up-dating late-breaking stories over the evening, and also drop in items of regional interest, by staying on the air five and one-half hours a night, ninety minutes in each time zone. (So long, Ontario and Quebec, hello, Manitoba.) In practice it proved to be an insane notion, ruinous to the pace of the program – not to mention our morale and health. It also meant that we played a lot of music while we waited for tardy guests to turn up, and our taste in discs was awful. No one wept when the roller-coaster was scrapped in favour of one ninety-minute package beamed out at the supper hour to every region of the country. But we do return to the format very occasionally, when special events like a budget or an election warrant. We did it, for example, for the 1974 British election, which is how Saskatchewan and Alberta got to hear Auberon Waugh do us in, live and unexpurgated.

Waugh, who is an editor of the British magazine *Private Eye*, and William Davis, the editor of *Punch*, were booked to provide analysis of that election, in which Harold Wilson's Labour party was unexpectedly returned to power. Once an hour Waugh and Davis would appear to give each successive time zone the latest results. What our witty pair did between stints was rush off in a waiting taxi to grab some sustenance at one of the election bashes in progress all over London.

By their fourth – and what they'd understood would be their last – inning for the night (after all, it was now 2:30 AM, London time), Davis and especially Waugh were not – let me put this kindly – as flexible as they might have been. The first they knew that they were expected back for one more round was the moment Alan Maitland thanked them for their fourth installment and bragged that our roller-coaster would now roll westward to the Pacific, where our guests would return to comment on what was just then becoming a very interesting race.

Waugh's mouth, we now know, moves faster than a technician's finger. Before we could close off the London mikes, the voice of Auberon Waugh came bellowing across the ocean, over the sleepy heads of Newfoundland and New Brunswick, onto the Prairies and into the foothills: "Like flying fuck we will. I'm going home."

For Saskatchewan, Alberta, and the Northwest Territories it was live and too late. British Columbia, however, could still be saved. But we would have to work fast to rebuild the program. With our guests in London long gone, with no one else at hand to talk about an election, and with only forty minutes left before we'd hit the Pacific zone, that was going to be complicated. Our technician was unleashed on the master tape to seek out and destroy one flying epithet and all references that might be out of date for the west-coast edition – not short work. And it wasn't finished when 6:30, BC time, came around. The hysterical solution was to throw on the air the first disc that came to hand. British Columbia, saved from obscenity, was assaulted instead by the heavy, raunchy throb of Led Zeppelin: "Baby, you make me sweat." In our panic we had compounded our calamity.

How to save it? There's an old bureaucratic maxim: never take responsibility; if necessary, blame others. Those who were listening that night now know why Alan Maitland, in his most regal tone, broke into Led Zeppelin to announce, "We interrupt local programming to bring you this special British Election Edition of As It Happens." Of course, it was our own debacle that we were interrupting, but until now no one has ever known.

Most of the interviews I've done over the past five years on radio are *not* in this book. Just as the program offers its listeners a selected sample of reality, so this book is a further narrowing down. Whole subject areas had to be left out. If you only knew *As It Happens* from this book, you might think that we never cared what the United States thinks about Allan Blakeney's potash policy, or what BC thinks of Quebec. Inevitably, the story that is most compelling when it's aired is the stalest and most irrelevant by the end of the week.

I've also had to leave out some great radio moments, because what made them great was mostly sound. The Russian poet Yevtushenko, for example, swept into my studio to read some poetry, which he did magnificently. But what made the encounter memorable was his lovely, lascivious voice. Now, when I read what we were actually saying to each other, it seems a little sillier than I would like to remember.

"That's about the dirtiest poem I've ever heard read on radio," I gulped. "My goodness, you weren't reading, you were kissing the microphone."

"Yes," whispered Yevtushenko, taking five caressing syllables to say the word. "Yes, because you are a woman, so I as a poet must protect you, my spiritual sister."

There have been a lot of moments like that. I remember them as magical. Then I read the transcript and decide to leave the experience in the forgiving fog of memory lane.

What I have included in this book are interviews that I hope read as well as they once played. If there is a general rationale it is summed up by this question: what does this conversation tell us about the way we are right now?

I've tried to keep the printed excerpts as close to the recorded interview as possible. I've also worked hard to preserve the flavour of the individual speaker. For smooth reading, however, I have edited, compressed, and clarified – which has left me with the largest collection of "ums," "ahs," false trails, and tangents in the world.

AS IT HAPPENED

One
Hiya Pope, Gotta Minute?
Chasing Down the News

No matter how you get it, the news is always a selection, a gerrymandered slice of reality. Your favourite newscaster signing off with " . . . and that's the news" is having you; "that's the news we've chosen to give you" would be more like it. Most of the world and its events are almost permanently ignored. Look at the way that Henry Kissinger "discovered" Africa recently, for instance; or the way Moluccan terrorists sent us scurrying for our atlases. How much do you really know about what's been happening lately in downtown Krakow?

Far from being a replica of the day's events, the news is a highly organized creation; you could even call it a distortion. In truth many sketches of the unfolding universe are possible, each containing only the information that a particular news team has wanted or has managed to get.

What we set out to get at *As It Happens* is decided by the democratic vote of our production staff. Out of the clash of different outlooks, backgrounds, and personal styles, we shape our show. And, let me tell you, it's a clash. We are in constant internal disagreement. In fact, the first clue that we are onto something good is the amount of argument a story suggestion will spark among ourselves.

What we don't argue about are certain general principles. We're always hard on phoney Canadian angles to international news, when the heart of a given story lies elsewhere. We don't cover political disputes as though the only interest in the world is Uncle Sam's. Angola, for example, was treated as a peripheral issue by most news outlets in Canada, until the deliberations of the American Congress made that African war an American story — and therefore Canadian front-page news. We're as interested in why a story is being leaked as in the story itself. And we always try to get to the people directly involved.

It's a wired world, as somebody has already noted, and we take advantage. If there are deep-sea divers under the ice at Frobisher Bay, you can be sure that they're not without a telephone. When a psychotic made an attempt on the life of Princess Anne, we had someone barge into the washroom at Scotland Yard to fetch to the telephone the woman who'd eyewitnessed the attack. We pursued to a lunch counter, where she'd retreated to compose herself, the girl who was standing next to Sara Jane Moore when that crazy lady took a pot-shot at Gerald Ford. I've even talked to a bank robber in the midst of his own hold-up.

A young man calling himself Cat was holding eleven hostages at a bank in Greenwich Village, New York City. He was demanding the release of Patty Hearst and her three SLA friends, plus a token something for his troubles — ten million in gold. We got the branch's number from the bank's head office and cut right by the army of battle-dressed policemen sealing off the area — right into the bank. The phone rang once, twice, a third time. Then a cheerful male voice came on the line.

"Hull-low."

"Hello," I chirped, guessing that this had to be the hold-up man; a hostage wouldn't sound so relaxed. "I'm calling for the Canadian Broadcasting Corporation —"

"Canada," he exulted. "Far out. How're ya doin' up there in Canada. It's cold, huh?"

"We'd like to know what's going on there," I said, briskly moving past the small talk. Obligingly, he got down to business.

"I've got eleven people here and I'm negotiating for Patty Hearst, the Harris's, and that oriental girl, plus ten million in gold. That's it," he signed off, dropping the phone onto its cradle.

Fortunately for a program dependent on it, bank robbers aren't the only people unable to leave a ringing phone alone. During the Cod War (Part One), the Icelanders, furious at Britain for fishing in what the Icelanders considered their territorial waters, spent their frustration in stoning the British embassy. We thought we'd try to get through to the embattled diplomats. Not only did we get through, the ambassador himself picked up the phone.

"I'd like to speak to the British ambassador," I announced.

"I am the ambassador," came the reply over the sound of shattering glass.

"We understand there's a riot going on," I said obtusely. "What is that terrible noise in the background?"

"My windows, Madame."

"Ambassador," I went on, "we'd like your view of the current dispute between your country and Iceland." The ambassador was now a little upset.

"My dear Madame," he ordered frostily, "will you please get off my line. I have to telephone my Foreign Office."

"Please, just one moment," I persisted. "I need only one comment – "

"Madame," he pleaded, now barely able to conceal the edge of hysteria creeping into his cultured tones, "Madame, you don't seem to understand. I haven't yet reported to my own government. There's only one line out of here, which you are rudely monopolizing."

I proposed a solution. "Well, if you'll just answer my one question, I'll be glad to leave you to your duties."

Having no choice, the poor man did. And that's how *As It Happens* listeners that night got to hear the views of a besieged British diplomat, with the sound of his own embassy being stoned in the background.

Before you conclude that *As It Happens* has infallible news sense, let me tell you that for days we laughed off the importance of a young heiress in San Francisco who'd been kidnapped in her bathrobe by urban guerillas. For the first forty-eight hours we had a good excuse – local journalists had agreed to honour a news blackout to help police. Yet even when the embargo was lifted, our producers insisted that there was little to it. While reporters from around the globe flew into San Francisco and while the front yard of Randolph Hearst's mansion turned into a media zoo of remote TV trucks, press tables, and pay phones nailed to the trunks of the trees, we kept playing down the reports of our stringer. Each day he would eagerly call from one of those pay phones, ready to give us what he was convinced was the tale of the decade. But each day we'd turn up our collective nose, disdaining just another California kook story.

I probably shouldn't tell you this, either, but the incredible coup of speaking to Mrs. Solzhenitsyn the night her husband was hustled out of the Soviet Union – a scoop which more than any other single accomplishment, I think, gave us national recognition – was no more than a lucky accident. When we learned of Solzhenitsyn's expulsion, we dialled the only number we had in Moscow that might be useful. It was a number where we had reached Andrei Sakharov a few times – not his home phone, but a special number at which he took calls of encouragement from the West on Wednesday afternoons. Solzhenitsyn was kicked out on a Tuesday, but the story producer dialled the Wednesday number, anyway.

By pure chance, he raised someone. The man in Moscow responded to our staffer's limited Russian (actually, all he did was scream the word "Sakharov" seven times into the receiver) with another number. That other number got us right into a meeting of the Russian dissident community. Solzhenitsyn's friends had gathered to compose a protest statement, which Sakharov first read to the world on our program. When he'd finished, I asked him how Mrs. Solzhenitsyn was taking this terrible event. "I don't know," he replied. "Why don't you ask her yourself?" Incredibly, we had reached the Solzhenitsyns' own apartment. Once again, it was proved that you don't have to be smart, as long as you're lucky.

I'm not quite sure what this proves, but after we got off

the phone to Moscow we called Canadian Press, the *Globe and Mail*, and the Toronto *Star*, offering each of them our tape. All three turned us down. Harrison Salisbury at the New York *Times*, on the other hand, gladly took it — which is how Canadian readers got Mrs. Solzhenitsyn's statements two days later, under a New York *Times* Service byline, giving *As It Happens* credit.

Because we don't have the manpower or the money to blanket a story or to cover everything that happens, we have to pick our places. That's how we came to take Woodward and Bernstein seriously, when a lot of listeners thought we were being obnoxious and perversely anti-American. That's why we did breakthrough work on the threat of chemical killers like arsenic, mercury, asbestos, and lead. And it explains the enthusiasm with which we wrestled New York State to the ground over the beaver to save that industrious rodent as the symbol of Canada.

But good luck and good judgment aren't all that's required in chasing down the news. Often just as crucial are all kinds of negative, limiting, frustrating forces. Some are as banal as a dinner invitation that takes a planned-for guest out instead of waiting for our call.

"Hello, is that Kampala?"

"Yes."

"Is that the residence of President Amin?"

"You are who?"

"We are calling from Canada for the Canadian Broadcasting Corporation."

"What is your name?"

"Barbara Frum."

"You are who?"

"Barbara Frum. Can you hear me?"

"Yes. What can I do for you?"

"We would like to speak to President Amin. He has offered to negotiate between the Irish protestants and Irish catholics and we would like to hear his plan."

"About the Arabs?"

"Not the Arabs today, the Irish."

"Ah, you make words, you make telegram, not the telephone. He is too busy. You send a telegram."

"Can you tell me this, please, has – "

"If you want him you make telegram to him."

[Click.]

A few months later Amin came to New York to address the United Nations General Assembly under the auspices of the Organization of African Unity. This time we came closer; an interview time was actually arranged. We called his suite at the Waldorf Astoria, but again Amin had stood us up. Or, as the general's aide put it to the disappointed story producer, "Sorry, no General Amin. He fokked off."

Sometimes a producer can use up a whole day like that. Other times you chase down an eyewitness, only to discover that he has completely forgotten what he saw. We can miss the story of the night because the coup or guerilla hijacking happens twenty minutes after the program is put to bed. We're limited, as well, by the competence of people on the scene to describe a given day's events, and by their capacity to make the story meaningful. After the 1976 Italian earthquake, for example, with hundreds dead, thousands homeless, whole communities destroyed, and plague in the offing, I asked a British major who was there doing relief work to describe the tragedy and horror he saw around him.

"How does it look to you," I asked, wanting to be subtle.

"Well, it's a broad plain that winds upwards into snow-capped mountains. One could say it's both plains and mountains."

Thanks, major.

During the last chaotic days of the Vietnam War, we were at the mercy of the Hong Kong telephone operators, who sometimes didn't feel like paging the Saigon bars at dawn looking for our correspondents. Actually, I prefer not to think how much our show is influenced by the caprices of long-distance operators. One night we tried to reach the Vatican, right after a French journalist had accused the pope of performing unnatural acts with an Italian movie star when Paul was still a bishop. We thought it only fair to offer His Holiness equal time.

"Operator," I said, "I want to call Vatican City, person-to-person, for Pope Paul."

"How do you spell that?"

"How do you — P-O-P-E P-A —

"Oh, *Pope Paul.* Are you a priest, a cardinal, a bishop, or what?"

By this time I had two operators, one in Rome and one in Montreal, both equally determined to protect the privacy of the pontiff. I never got past them.

As hard as we try to report only what is true, there's no reporter who doesn't occasionally get caught by invented news. Once, a memo from our London office suggested that we might want to do a piece sometime on how Heathrow Airport protects itself against terrorists. By the time that idea had been relayed through three different staffers to a new and very keen story producer, it had become a hot tip: the IRA was about to attack Heathrow. Naively, the producer checked out the details by calling a colleague at the London *Daily Mirror*.

"We just learned that the IRA is about to launch a missile attack against Heathrow," he probed.

"Really," said the *Daily Mirror*, and promptly alerted Scotland Yard.

Two days later, after we'd all forgotten the incident, our copy of the London *Times* arrived with this front-page story: tipped off by "sources" in Canada, the British Army took defensive action today at Heathrow. That was one credit we have never wanted to claim.

Sometimes news can be distorted by plain old niceness, by a guest who wants to shield you from reality and so gives you what he thinks you want to hear. I had a wonderful chat with the author of a new book about David Livingstone, the man whom Stanley presumed to find. He gave us a lovely interview, full of anecdote and quotation from the book. But the man on the phone in London, we later discovered, wasn't the author at all; he was the critic who had reviewed the book. He'd been so anxious to protect us from our silly mistake that he did the whole interview without once letting on. He even had an answer when I asked why he'd done the book — "Because I felt it needed doing."

His goodness was to go unrewarded. When he asked our London office for payment for appearing, he was politely informed that the CBC never pays authors who come on radio programs to push their own books. We only pay those who talk for a living, like journalists and critics.

They say that courtroom lawyers never ask a question that they don't know the answer to. For me, the point of interviewing has always been the opposite. Where's the excitement or the fun if there are no surprises? Depending on the story I'm trying to get, I see myself as catalyst, watchdog, editor, or straightperson. I'm there to encourage the exhausted correspondent in Beirut and convince him not to protect us from the butchery he's seen. Even more, I think, I'm there to push the correspondent in Angola who apparently hasn't gone downtown to check out reports that millions of dollars worth of Soviet weapons are being unloaded at the dock; but from his hotel room can miraculously follow the machinations of CIA mercenaries hundreds of miles away in Zaire.

I was called down by a guest once for pushing too hard. The interview was about the blackmailing of illegal immigrants in British Columbia, and my guest was accusing the Mounties of harassment. Yet, when I pressed him to spell out the particulars, he got upset.

"You know, the thing about your interviews, Barbara, is – and I often listen to *As It Happens* – it's a bit like you're asking for bread and circuses. You're asking me to come across with new, groovy information that you haven't heard before. And you keep saying, 'What proof do you have.' Well, you know, it's very hard to prove these things."

"I just want you to understand," I tried to explain, "that for the audience to believe you, you've got to sound credible."

"Do I sound like a madman?" he huffed.

"No," I said, "it's not what you sound like. It's whether the audience will believe you."

"Well, everyone I meet – " he persisted.

I had to interrupt.

"That's the point. The audience doesn't see you. They just hear you, okay? I'm just trying to help you because if you can't make a case, your whole story will be dismissed."

I'm certain that people who have a good case sound more convincing when they're up against a strong questioner.

And besides, I love the match. I strain for the dropped hint, the unspoken fear, the whisky on the breath, the edge of anger or nervousness that might give me an in. Every nuance is crucial when listening is all you've got. There are no eyes across the table to warn you, no body language giving you easy cues. The listener, too, is obliged to do without the easy signals like age and class and manner, which normally short-circuit judgment. You can only deal with what is said. Hearing a telephone conversation over the radio seems to add a special tension and crackle. Perhaps the excitement comes from the forced marriage of the cool, impersonal phone to the intense, intimate medium of radio. Perhaps it's the mix of my controlled, journalist tone and the relaxed, more conversational style of guests. Or it could be simply that people love to eavesdrop and *As It Happens* is like listening in on a wiretap — except it's legal.

Maybe because I've been doing it for so long, pursuing the news over the telephone instead of face to face has come to seem full of all kinds of advantages, too. When you say "Goodby" on the telephone, you just press your little red de-conferencing button and your guest disappears forever. What chances an interviewer can take when he's hundreds, maybe thousands of miles away! I'd never thought very deeply about that until one of our producers went to California to book a special series of interviews for the program. He reported to me later how it felt to be on the receiving end. One of the interviews that he'd lined up was with S. I. Hayakawa, the feisty former president of San Francisco State College. Apparently, Hayakawa was ready for a "How quiet the campus is today" kind of interview; I was doing a "Don't you now regret it, didn't you maybe over-react" interview, instead.

The producer in California, who could see and hear Hayakawa only, began feeling queasy as Hayakawa's eyes narrowed and his knuckles tightened around the phone. In my poor colleague's mind's eye was another vision: the little red button on the telephone in Toronto, that little red button that he himself had gleefully pressed so many times. This time, when it was pressed in Toronto, he would be abandoned in the same room with a very angry educator.

"Knee-jerk liberal," fumed Hayakawa as he slammed down the receiver. "That's just the kind of interviewer I hate."

"Yes," agreed the terrified producer, backing away. "I was hoping for a better airing of the subject myself."

Two
The Conspiracy

I heard it first from Sergeant Jack Burbridge of the Ottawa detachment; later I got it from the commissioner himself: the Royal Canadian Mounted Police Force loves *As It Happens*. They love it so much that they've actually assigned officers in the Intelligence Branch to tape and transcribe every word of ours that goes out over the air. Now, I'm inclined to accept that as a compliment, although some of my friends at the CBC tend to see it otherwise. They walk around convinced that the RCMP is so enthusiastic about our show – and the people who produce it – that the Mounties tune in on us, even when we're not on the air.

That's a bit paranoid, of course. But then who isn't a little suspicious lately? Given the run of intrigues, cabals, and scenarios we're living through, it's not hard to understand why even the most innocent events are being scanned for hidden meaning; or why suggestions that five years ago would have been dismissed as ludicrous now get a knowing, "Yeah, I can believe that."

I liked it better the old way, when you could sort the reasonable from the unreasonable by deciding what was likely and had a good chance of being right; when you could still trust gut instinct about what people would do and how far they'd go. Now, experience and intuition seem useless –

27

destroyed, maybe forever, in a flood of the most unlikely, unbelievable stories.

Just consider the tales we've heard lately, each adding a few more doubts to the pile of suspicion already there: the RCMP is playing politics, trying to bring down Trudeau by leaking documents embarrassing to his government; the CIA provided the fronts and conduits through which Lockheed Aircraft corrupted half the elected governments in the world; Bernardine Dohrn of the Weather Underground has become a big-time weapons dealer, supplying arms to her comrades in the Irish and Angolan wars. It wasn't four weeks after the daring raid against OPEC headquarters in Vienna before we were told that the kidnapping was actually a plot of three Arab states against the others, and that Carlos the Jackal is not a revolutionary freelancer at all but the striking arm of Libya's Colonel Kadhafi.

But how do you make sense of anything anymore when a President of the United States will accept the gift of a callgirl from his buddy Frank Sinatra and unconcernedly share her with a Mafia big-shot – who, in turn, has taken a contract from the CIA to bump off the President's Cuban embarrassment, Fidel Castro – with a poisoned cigar, no less? Is it any wonder that even the most conservative journalists now report on international affairs as if political life were cast with as many gangsters as an old Humphrey Bogart movie? Every day it seems to get a little bit harder to pick out the paranoid nuts from the sensible Jeremiahs.

One evening a Toronto art teacher showed up at the studio armed with a professional magnifying glass and his new Eaton's mail-order catalogue, anxious to expose to the *As It Happens* audience the fact that, beyond all the laws of probability, the letters S and E and X were scattered throughout the pages of that venerable institution's catalogue. The word SEX was in every picture, but especially clustered on the skin of the catalogue models – cheeks, bosoms, necks – even the innocent foreheads of small children were sullied.

Like all conspiracy buffs, our teacher was intense and troubled, and perhaps I should now apologize for indulging in frivolity; especially because, two days later, in the afternoon mail there was this communication from a worried Calgary listener:

> I refuse to believe in the Great Conspiracy but sometimes I get a trifle scared. I think you might be interested in the enclosed picture.

The accompanying photo was a full-page, colour shot of *me* torn from *Maclean's* Magazine – and damn if it wasn't riddled with the letters s and e and especially x in the most devilishly subliminal way. That most-established Peter C. Newman part of The Conspiracy? Migawd – now, that really is too much.

After five years and dozens of conspiracy buffs, I've concluded that the test for quality in any conspiracy theory is the presence and use of the "Rockefeller Interests," or simply Nelson Rockefeller. As in: we have evidence that the CIA is the private militia of the Rockefeller Interests; or, our present economic bind started the night that Nelson Rockefeller began filching the gold bars out of Fort Knox. I know that sounds crazy, but you'd be amazed how uncrazy the characters who tell such fables sound. There's even a shadowy figure in New York City who has convinced a zealous band of followers (including branch-plant cadres in Toronto, Montreal, and Vancouver) that world power is being consolidated at this very moment under a clandestine alliance of the KGB, the CIA, and the British Secret Service – all of whom are taking their orders from you-know-who, of course.

I myself received a frantic telegram labelled "Personal and Confidential" on the eve of the last British Columbia election:

> Suggest you interview Labour party immediately. There are underlying reasons for desperation as D. Barrett may be an agent of US banking interests.

That Rockefeller – what a devil!

As intriguing as the Rockefeller scenarios are, my choice for the most creative conspiracy package, and certainly the tidiest, is the one offered by American writer Carl Oglesby, former SDS president, now a teacher at MIT. In one artful construction under the title "Yankees and Cowboys," he takes a tangle of confusing events and weaves intrigues, plots, and counterplots into one breathtaking tapestry. His theory, which we explored in this interview, is a classic of contemporary conspiracy art — vivid, daring, and not designed for close scrutiny.

Let me take a stab at what you seem to be saying, Mr. Oglesby. The Cowboys did in the Yankees at Dallas, so the Yankees did in the Cowboys at Watergate?

> It goes a little further than that. That's the rhythm of it, but there are some intervening doings-in. Let's follow it your way. The Yankees do the Cowboys in with some trickery in the 1960 national elections, involving the Daley machine in Illinois and the Johnson machine in Texas. In other words, it's not altogether clear that Jack Kennedy won the election in 1960. People on the Nixon side believe that Kennedy stole the election. Given that, and other provocations — Vietnam, Cuba, *et cetera* — the Cowboys return the favour in 1963.

But just hold it right there. The Cowboys now get Johnson. Obviously, Johnson is a Cowboy.

> Oh, yeah.

How can he be part of the Nixon thing? He's a Democrat.

> You can't follow the fight if you think it's a fight between two parties. There are larger forces here, profoundly organized, that employ the two parties as a means of tempering their differences and preserving a unified framework.

And the assassination of John Kennedy — how does that fit in?

> Just to tell the whole bloody story in a single sentence, it seems that there's strong circumstantial evidence to support the view that a Cowboy group was infuriated at Jack Kennedy in 1961 for stopping them at the Bay of Pigs, because Kennedy wouldn't let them have the air support they had counted on and left them stranded to become humiliated. They were further infuriated at certain adventures to the left that Kennedy started to take in 1962 and 1963, and therefore blew him away in Dallas

in order to get their man on top and to get a big-war policy installed in respect to Vietnam. There's quite a solid record substantiating the view that Kennedy was reversing Vietnam escalation in 1963, so they blew him away.

Okay, hang on. Who's "they," then? Who blew him away?

There's an argument whether there were four or five people shooting at Kennedy. Oswald was apparently not one of them. So it's like who pulled the trigger, who organized it, who staged it, who worked it out? A lot of people are suggesting that Howard Hunt casts a shadow in this business. I mean, there are some interesting facts. For example, Nixon was in Dallas on November twenty-second, on the morning of the very day that Kennedy arrived there to get killed. Yet when somebody asked him where he was, he didn't remember. He thought he was maybe in an airplane someplace.

He was on Pepsi-Cola business, wasn't he?

Well, he says so. Except that a guy by the name of Richard Sprague, who was associated with Fensterwald, who was connected with McCord — if you like daisy chains — has now got evidence showing that there was no such meeting of Pepsi. But what really makes it striking is that he should have fumbled it. How could he not know that he was in Dallas the morning Kennedy was killed? He doesn't go to Dallas that much in his life.

And you think that there's a link between Watergate and the assassination of Kennedy.

I think there is. I expect real strong evidence to turn up pretty soon that there is a group that we have to call the Sinister Force. That's what Haig called it, if you re-member, when he was asked how the eighteen and a half minutes got wiped off the tape. He said, "There must be some Sinister Force." So now we're like good scientists who hypothesize something. Now we must start trying to track it down. We can't expect to see it all at once, right out in front of us.

But you say you can see a link. What's the link?

Well, don't push that too fast. One can easily overstate the case, you see. It's very easy for these ideas to be discredited at this point. Saying too much is like inviting a frost.

But Watergate?

Okay. What happened at Watergate was that Yankees employed clandestine methods to blow Cowboy Nixon out of the water, when his policy extravagance exceeded Yankee tolerances, especially with respect to Nixon's economic policy.

If Watergate was a Yankee plot in retaliation for Dallas, how could they manage to use Cowboys against themselves?

That involves the question of McCord. I think McCord is a Yankee agent in the Cowboy inner camp, exfiltrated from the CIA, falsely retired in 1970. I don't even know how to deal with this idea that he was not a CIA officer in the Watergate operation, in the break-in and in the bust. There's no way he could not have been CIA. He's CIA up one side and down the other.

And what about Ford?

Ford is a long-time — I can't call him a Yankee agent or a Rockefeller agent, but let's just say he's been very close to the Rockefellers and all their world.

How, then, do you account for a figure like Henry Kissinger, who seems to be equally acceptable to both sides? What does that do to your theory?

It shows that this, after all, is a functioning arrangement. Sure, Kissinger is a good Yankee type. Kissinger is, so to speak, a ministerial ambassador from the Chase Manhattan Empire, imposed on Nixon. And the reason that happened was that Nixon wasn't strong enough to govern without including Rockefeller in an inner seat. And we still didn't get around to talking about the killing of King and of Bobby Kennedy, which also move in this narrative. As does the unhorsing of Johnson, if you remember that — when he decided to retire rather than face a defeat. You can see Yankee gunslingers all over that one — Clark Clifford, Averell Harriman, Cyrus Vance, George Ball. The Yankees send their heavies to get something done. Then, pretty soon — zap, almost April Fool's — Johnson comes on and says he's going to stop the bombing and he's not going to run. And the next thing that happens is that Martin Luther King bites the dust. Move, countermove, countermove, counter, counter. Along comes Bobby Kennedy with his meteoric campaign and starts sweeping everybody away. And then bang, bang — it's LA. Want to know why people don't get into this stuff more?

Okay.

Because the picture is here. It's right in front of us. When we accept the implications of the idea that Jack Kennedy was not killed by the lone Oswald and the implications of the cover-up for all these years, then, hypothetically at least, we're looking at a kind of corruption in government that's too sickening to even confront or discuss, much less do something about.

A conservative way of coping with The Conspiracy — certainly the way of William F. Buckley, Jr. — is to deny its existence. Buckley had come to the CBC studios in New York City to talk to me about his experiences as a delegate to the United Nations. At the end of that interview I couldn't resist asking what he thought about the succession of pratfalls, CIA dirty tricks, and general foul-ups which had been plaguing the folks on Pennsylvania Avenue, the same folks who had appointed him to the UN mission. Buckley himself had worked for the CIA in his younger days, during a time when that agency's motto, "And ye shall know the truth and the truth shall make you free," didn't make people want to squirm. It was at the CIA that he'd become friends with Nixon's plumber, E. Howard Hunt, for example.

Why I thought I'd get a useful insight on the issue of paranoia from Bill Buckley I don't know. Buckley is the master of the obfuscating, complexifying, convulstiforming sentence. His words and phrases are like gooey caramel; they pour over you, suffocating you till you can't even breathe anymore — never mind remember where you wanted to go with your next question. This time, to my amazement, he was almost brusque. He rebuffed my probes about government conspiracy, insisting, with his traditional open-mindedness, that the only conspiracy worth the name was of the Left-wing variety.

His pique is understandable, of course. After all, the Right had been digging out the Communist Conspiracy for years, unthanked. Buckley revels in his role as the exquisite lance of the investigators. He wasn't about to let some Canadian interviewer cast him as defender of the investigated. As you read the exchange, keep in mind that we talked in mid-December of 1974, exactly five days before the New York *Times* broke the news of CIA domestic spying and all the embarrassing skeletons came tumbling out of that agency's overstuffed closets – assassination plots against foreign leaders, poison-dart guns, underworld links, news correspondents as secret agents, break-ins, intercepted telegrams, manipulation of foreign elections – you name it, the CIA was into it.

Mr. Buckley, how do you protect yourself against paranoia – the feeling that the spooks are everywhere? Are you prone to that sort of worrying?

I'm not even aware of these worries.

I can't believe it. You must not read.

Well, I read a great deal, but maybe I don't read kook stuff as much as you do, Miss Frum. If you can give me an example from any magazine that I've ever heard of, maybe that will make it more familiar to me.

I'm not talking about death rays from the skies. I'm talking about very middle-of-the-road journals and I'm talking about ordinary people who feel there are too many unanswered questions.

Well, that was a concern of the Romans two thousand years ago, and has been a concern in America and in Canada and in every country in the world that I know of. You can't travel into the most pastoral corner of the world without running into somebody who thinks that the CIA was responsible for the latest municipal results in the city of Gstaad.

What about this, then. Julie Nixon, the former president's own daughter, is even hinting that Watergate was actually a counterplot committed by forces out there that Nixon had been battling. At least that's what she's implying.

Oh, I think that's true.

And what were the forces out there?

Utter and total disruption of democratic mechanisms. Anyone who was around during the passionate years here knows that civil liberties were definitely threatened. The ecologists wouldn't allow any dissent in Harvard University. You couldn't have a seminar in which somebody was permitted to speak on the side of the Vietnam War. Deans were thrown into the river. Seventy thousand bombs were exploded in 1969. Students were killed.

Do you think there was an organized conspiracy behind that?

Of course it's organized. How in the hell do you get half a million people marching to Washington without organizing it?

But who was behind it, do you think? What kind of forces?

Well, we know who was behind it; ministers, baby doctors, Soviet agents, everybody — there was a little bit of everything in it.

And the FBI and the CIA — are they Sinister Forces, too?

Look, I have heard it said that the CIA decided to stage Watergate in order to overthrow Nixon. Now, I've heard that and a lot of other silly things said in my life and I'll hear a lot of sillier things before I die. I think that you simply have to test those theses up against the plausibilities. The fact is that it wasn't the Watergate burglary that did Nixon in, it was his behaviour after it — and that couldn't have been predicted by CIA. So I think, really, that's a lot of stuff and nonsense. Very, very few people believe in it, although it's true that in all societies the idea of a conspiracy is appealing.

Boy, we're going to sleep safer in our beds tonight after talking to you.

Right. Very nice talking to you, Miss Frum.

The fact that American intelligence didn't interfere in the latest municipal elections in Gstaad I find immensely reassuring. I only wish that those agencies had comparable qualms about involving themselves in domestic matters here. In 1975 a number of stories broke that suggested that the forty-ninth parallel might not be a boundary line on the maps of the FBI or CIA. The issue quickly – and rightly – became a question of national dignity as much as national sovereignty. It was bad enough to have foreign agents snooping on Canadian citizens on Canadian soil with the knowledge and approval of our own government. It was a scandal if they were doing so without.

Joseph Burton, a forty-two-year-old Floridian, claims he was sent by the FBI to infiltrate Maoists in Ontario and Quebec in order to spy on them. He says that he did it, from 1972 to 1974, without the knowledge of our government. Now, police forces confronted with accusations like that tend to deny them, and count on the majority of us to give the authorities the benefit of the doubt. Unfortunately, benefit-of-the-doubt is another beleaguered concept. Hardly anyone believes denials anymore.

Mr. Burton, could I establish this first, please? Did the Canadian government or Canadian intelligence people know that you were operating in Canada for the FBI?

I understand, from information given to me by my superior in the FBI, that the Canadian government did not know who I was, would not know me if they saw me, did not know when I was there, and only got a synopsis report of my activities – or rather what the FBI considered important for them – after I had returned to the US. I had no contact with your RCMP or your intelligence division. In fact, only seven people in the intelligence division of the FBI knew about this operation, so it was not a widely known operation.

Was part of the reason for that secrecy the fact that the FBI is not supposed to operate outside the United States?

Let me say this to you. My immediate supervisor once told me in 1973 that if what we were doing ever got out, it would be the Watergate of the FBI. To quote him, and I'll put this in closed quotes, "Joe, be very careful. If this ever gets out, it will be the Watergate of the bureau."

You say that you spoke out about the FBI in Canada because there was an ethical factor in this, because "the Canadians are totally capable of looking after themselves."

Yes, that's correct. You see, although the Canadians did not know who I was specifically and personally, they realized from information that they were getting from the FBI that the FBI was operating in Canada.

How? I don't understand?

Because if I know every pot and pan in your kitchen, I must have been in your kitchen, right?

Do you think the FBI was in liaison with intelligence people here, reporting back what you were finding out?

Most definitely. In fact, the Canadian intelligence division, through the FBI, gave me an invitation to come up and spend a few months in Canada to work with them. I declined that invitation.

While you were operating in Canada, did you ever worry about getting picked up by Canadian authorities?

Yes. It was clearly understood that if I was picked up in Canada, I would have been picked up in Canada. In other words, there was nobody to run to or nobody to call. This is part of the operation.

Were you ever afraid that the RCMP might be told that the FBI was operating in Canada and that your cover would be blown?

No. I was assured by the FBI — and this I can give you a direct answer to — that no one in the Canadian intelligence division, the RCMP, and absolutely no locals, you know — because they're rather on the low end of the ladder — would ever know my identity. In other words, if they picked me up, they would have picked me up as a Marxist-Leninist from Florida. You see, the name that was used for me in the bureau was not Joseph A. Burton.

Why send you? Why don't American agencies rely on Canadian intelligence people? Why don't they just make requests?

I think you'd have to ask them that. I think they simply would rather rely on their own direct intelligence information than barter with Canada for it. They expressed very clearly that I was obtaining information and estab-

lishing closer contact and better ability to disrupt or-
ganizations — better than Canadian operators had ever
been able to do, evidently. Why else would they want a
US citizen to come to Canada and work for them?
Were you led to believe you were the only FBI agent operating in this country?
No, I knew I wasn't. I had another one with me at times.
I mean, separate missions that wouldn't intersect with
yours?
They would not have told me that. We operate on a
need-to-know basis and I would not have needed to know
that.
Do you feel in any danger now? The FBI is going to be pretty
furious with you. And what about the groups you were
spying on?
Well, in the case of the bureau, I'm taking a very con-
stitutional position. I think we're too far down the road
for me to worry about the bureau at this point. Earlier, I
was concerned, but they couldn't do anything now. It
would be too apparent. As far as the Left goes, I would
say that retaliation from the bureau would be a greater
fear to me over the longer period of time than any
retaliation from the Left would be.

Ottawa journalist Bill MacAdam believes that intelligence people in Canada and the US sometimes do odd jobs
together without telling anybody — not even the politicians
they're responsible to. In the still-mysterious events at the
Cuban Trade Mission in Montreal during the night of April
4, 1972, for example, MacAdam sees the combined talents of
the CIA and our own beloved Mounties.

Mr. MacAdam, are you sure?
We were definitely involved. It was low-level co-
operation between the CIA and the Canadian people, but
it went against government policy. A senior person in
External Affairs told me that if it had gone for a policy
decision, it would never have been cleared.
What part did we actually play in it? What did we do?
It was a staged break-in, with our co-operation. Al-

though, in this particular case, it went against government policy and in no way was in our interest.

What is the deal between us? Do we work with them because we have no choice or because we get something back?

We get enormous amounts of information from the National Security Agency. We also have access to all the
computers at the NSA, which is the largest-budgeted
intelligence arm of the United States, so we have access
to this very sophisticated technology.

The thing I'm so curious about is that when there's something really tricky to be done, do they trust us to pull our
weight or do they just ignore our sovereignty and go ahead
on their own?

In most cases they trust us to pull our weight, and we do.
There are other cases where the CIA has tried to run
agents in Canada and they've been found out. All hell
broke loose. But in most cases, if the CIA wants to run an
agent in Canada, they simply say so to the security
service of the RCMP. He's run by the security service of
the RCMP for the CIA. Just as in Cuba, after the United
States left Cuba, the CIA agents were taken over mainly
by the British, and some by the Canadians.

Do the Americans give us things we need, or is it a one-way
street?

Much of it is useless, that's the point. We get a whole
mass of information that we cannot possibly digest or
use. There's no question about that. The whole intelligence thing is being overvalued right now. It's got completely out of hand, and it's not being controlled by the
policy-makers. The attitude seems to be that if you can
get a bit of information, it doesn't matter how you get it.
All the while we are thinking we're independent in international affairs — peace-makers and so on — which is
nonsense. The only people who are being hoodwinked
that we're independent are the people in this country.
Everybody else knows what we're doing.

What I try to keep alert for when I'm faced with an
interview about corporate intrigue or political connivance is

what my colleague Patrick Keatley of the *Guardian* calls the Siberian Sleighride Technique – when you're trying to save your skin and are being chased by wolves, keep chucking bits of meat over the side to distract your pursuers, and maybe you'll keep riding a bit longer. An awful lot of meat has gone over the side recently – a Royal Dutch chunk from Lockheed Aircraft, some well-fed executives from Gulf, and a bevy of Italian, Canadian, and Japanese bureaucrats.

The late Howard Hughes used the technique, reportedly, when his mystery ship the *Glomar Explorer* stopped being a mystery and became a scandal. As the story goes, Hughes' cronies at the CIA financed him with $300 million in government funds, to build a ship with the ability to work on the ocean floor. As part of the Watergate fallout, Congress was asking why.

Plunk went the first piece of meat: the *Glomar* was built to mine manganese nodules from the ocean and give the US a secret headstart on deep-sea mineral exploration. That explanation didn't stop the questioning for long. A second piece was carved off: okay, the ship was built to raise a drowned Russian nuclear submarine in order to learn its codes and secrets. That was more satisfying – for a while. The last we heard is that maybe the *Glomar* wasn't created to salvage at all, but rather to plant nuclear missiles under the sea, safe from Soviet detection and retaliation. Which version is the real story? Are any of them true? It could take thirty years before we know.

That's how long it took us conspiracy buffs to get one of the more disillusioning tales of corporate amorality I've ever heard. Bradford Snell, Assistant Counsel to the American Senate's Monopoly and Anti-Trust Sub-committee, used recently de-classified documents about American corporations in Europe during World War Two to show that what's good for General Motors hasn't necessarily been good for a lot of us, for a very long time.

What have you found out about GM in Germany during the war, Mr. Snell?

> Well, basically that General Motors, due to its extensive investments in the German economy, became an integral factor in the industrial life of pre-World-War-Two Germany. As a consequence of its investments there, it

became an integral part of the preparations for war, 1939 through 1941.

Among themselves, did GM people ever talk about conflicting loyalties at that time?

Not in the data that we've reviewed. It seems as if once you have an extensive amount of investments in a country, be it Nazi Germany or the United States, that investment requires you to take certain actions favourable to the government. In other words, their debt to the country requires them to become a major part of defence effort, or a major part of territorial ambitions, or even world conquest.

How big a help, for example, were they to the Axis powers?

A terrific help. In the mid-1930s you have General Motors and Standard Oil of New Jersey, through a joint venture, establishing synthetic fuel plants in Germany, without which, according to some captured Nazi war documents, World War Two would have been unthinkable. There is the establishment in 1936 of the largest military truck facility in Germany, the sole function of which was to manufacture Opel Blitz military trucks for the Wehrmacht. And finally, in 1939, GM converted the world's largest integrated automobile facility to warplane production. During the course of World War Two, that single facility produced the aircraft engines for 50 per cent of the Luftwaffe's most important medium-range bombers.

I assume most Americans who were shareholders in General Motors at that time did not know this?

I suspect they had absolutely no knowledge whatsoever as to what was going on.

Do you think that their dividends benefited from the activities in Germany?

From what I can determine, all of the wartime profits enjoyed by General Motors' German companies were retained in Germany, and after the war they were reinvested in the Opel automobile works.

General Motors was in a position to know a great deal about things inside Nazi Germany and could have told the American government about them — and vice versa.

Certainly a company that important to two belligerents

would have certain information, perhaps even more information than either of the two belligerents, because they'd be right in the middle. They'd have access to data that either side would certainly want. They may be in a position to trade information to ensure the security of their installations. And that's really the problem. They become, if not willing participants, captives. In order to preserve their properties from expropriation, they're willing to comply with any government decrees or orders.

Yet a multinational like this, I'm sure, would insist that it doesn't get involved in politics.

I know, but I think it's inevitable. I don't think it's a question of malevolent executives, but rather it's a question of entering a structural bind. Once you've become a major factor in a country, it's really irrevocable.

Did anyone try to punish GM after the war?

No, definitely not. Again, if you're working at the State Department and you find evidence like this, and at the same time realize that General Motors (and Detroit) is the major backbone of the American defence interest, what do you do? You're at the mercy of the company involved. And GM was a major factor in our defence effort.

And then you get into the incredible irony that, after the war, GM thought it deserved reparations for Allied bombing of its plants in Germany.

That is incredible. They sought and received thirty-three million dollars in reparations from the American government for Allied bombing, that is, the bombing by Allied planes of German war planes owned by General Motors.

And they got it.

They got it. The only question was whether or not General Motors had exaggerated the extent of the damage by Allied bombing.

Was there any resistance to paying GM that kind of money?

None whatsoever.

What about today? Do you see the multinational company as a force for peace now, as the companies would have you see them?

Well, I think in essence they're not a force for peace and they're not a force for war. They're essentially a force for profit and a force for their own private interests. The extent to which that diverges from the national interest of any country is really immaterial to them. And that's the danger that this whole thing poses, that essentially we have sovereign economic states making policy that affects the interests of several nations at a time. And yet these nations have no control over them whatsoever.

Because they're sovereign states of their own?

That's correct. I like to look at it this way. If General Motors were a country and you considered its sales as revenue (thirty-six billion dollars in 1975), it would be the third largest country in the world after the United States and the Soviet Union.

We will have to call you back again someday about Ford.

They were certainly involved in Nazi Germany investments, too. But General Motors calls the shots in the auto industry, and to that extent I think they're the leader in this area. And the point is that had the Nazis won, General Motors would have appeared impeccably Nazi. As Hitler began to lose, the company was able to re-emerge impeccably American. Either way, the corporation and the interest of its stockholders would have been preserved.

With spooks and snoops now such a regular feature on the political landscape, spying thrives as one of the last growth industries in a no-growth world. I've spoken to one of the biggies in that field a couple of times on *As It Happens*. His name is Martin Kaiser, and he's the guy to know at Martin Kaiser, Inc., in Timonium, Maryland. Kaiser manufactures and markets listening and anti-listening devices to everybody who's anybody in the spy field. One of his hot-sellers is an electronic transmitter, miniaturized down to a quarter-inch cube. Embedded in a toothbrush, for example, it can relay anything said in normal conversation – within a fifty-to-sixty-foot radius – to a receiver half a block away.

This conversation with Kaiser took place the day after he appeared as a witness before the US House Select Committee on Intelligence in 1975, to add what he could to revelations of illegal electronic snooping on American citizens by the CIA. I have a hunch that Kaiser was still reeling from that Congressional grilling because, in mid-interview, this usually cocky merchant of electronic wizardry suddenly asked *me* if I knew in whose interest it might be to have us all so paranoid. The thought was no more than an aside, really, but in those two or three revealing moments, Kaiser showed what conspiracy fever can do to the most cynical. Even Kaiser, supplier to the players, is wondering if he is just a helpless pawn in some master game.

Hi, Mr. Kaiser. You remember us, I hear.

> How can I forget you? You told me you were the sexiest broad in Canada.

You remembered that? It must be a year since we last spoke. You've got a very good memory.

> No. Just a lot of good tapes.

You mean you taped our last conversation? You're really into this paranoia game.

> Nah. I'm in it because it's what I do best, oddly enough. It's what I do best.

Doesn't it bother you to realize that your government clients have been using your devices to pick up a lot of scurrilous stuff instead of focusing on the bad guys? It's like Lyndon Johnson all over again – reading the bugging transcripts, courtesy of Hoover, for some titillating bedtime browsing.

> Look, when I go to any given agency, I ask them for technical parameters. I don't really get a chance to figure out what's going on in their devious little minds.

But you must wonder sometimes.

> No, not really. I really don't. That's probably why I survive in this business, by not wondering why or what. And that's why, when these revelations come out, I just shrug my shoulders. It doesn't excite me. Watergate didn't excite me. And the fact that the FBI buys my equipment through fronts doesn't excite me. To me it's all life, a yard wide. My job is to build a piece of electronic circuitry that performs a function.

And where they put your little cubes – do your clients ever tell you that?

Nope. And that's good. That's a piece of information that I don't want.

Does the RCMP buy from you through fronts, the way the FBI does?

No, no. They're a very straightforward customer. Their primary interest is in the area of counterintelligence, to protect your national security. These are just normal defensive devices and any responsible government has to have them. You can't stop another government from listening to yours unless you have them, although I'm not saying that we do that to Canada. That's just a fact of life. Having this type of equipment just shows that Canadian intelligence is in the twenty-first century instead of the twentieth century.

How good is your quarter-inch cube? What can it do?

I could get really dramatic and say that it can make or break governments or something like that. But it's a good little transmitter. It's as small as I've seen any realistic devices manufactured, which is moderately small. You're going to have to come down here and see how we do this kind of stuff. Then you'd have a better feel for what's going on out here in this real world of manufacturing.

If you will sell to police agencies, presumably they are interested in who else you're selling to. Are you watchers being watched too, do you think?

I don't know whether I am or not. That's irrelevant. You have to visualize me like a workhorse. I'm too busy pulling the load to worry about the flies behind my tail-end. If people want to watch — great. That's more fun. But I don't really care. I have a very important job to do and I do it as best I can. I'm not in the paranoid game. I'm in the real-life, nitty-gritty, firing-bullets-at-each-other game. And I'd like to think that every surveillance device I make is being used for lawful purposes. Those are the standards of the game I play by.

That's funny. Know what's happened to me since our last conversation?

What?

I've been thinking that maybe I'm losing my sense of outrage. The eavesdropping mentality has just become part of the landscape. People like you and the things you make – I mean, we've all accepted it. Maybe because the temptations are just so great.

That's why the most important thing is not the hardware, because the hardware can be duplicated by anybody. But it's having the little devious nature to stay one step ahead, or a little bit better than the rest of the stuff coming down the pipe. And that's why, from the design standpoint, I never sit still. It's basically a cat-and-mouse game. You design a new surveillance device and then you design the equipment to find it. And then you out-design your first device with new countermeasure equipment. And it just goes on and on. In the area of intelligence and counterintelligence, there's no stopping point. There's no point that you can ever reach and say, "The field is filled."

It's a growth industry.

That's right, forever.

I thought Watergate meant a change in morality in your country?

Oh, no. I just think we're doing it to each other a little bit better than we did in the past, that's all. You know, Barbara, this is one of the things that Roosevelt stated: if anything happens in life, you can be damn sure that it was planned to happen that way. And I look at this game sometimes and I wonder, who the heck is running the game plan? Is he doing this to create employment, or is he doing this to create general paranoia, or is he doing this to upgrade law enforcement? What the heck game plan is he playing by? I don't know and it just baffles me.

Every time I talk to you I get so depressed that I make up my mind I'll never talk on the phone again.

I wish you luck. What I say is, let's do it like the Japanese. Let's live with it. The rule of life I'd recommend is: just assume everything you say is public knowledge, regardless of the confidentiality involved.

But what a way to live!

That's the only way. The Japanese do it and they get along perfectly. They accept it as standard operating procedure, and if we did that, too, I think everyone

would be an awful lot happier. Does that sound like a
piece of philosophy?
Yeah . . . . And what about you? Got any interesting com-
missions you can talk about?
   Sure. There are a few things. I'd go so far as to say that.
   You have very good intelligence up there in Canada.
No, it's you and your FBI. You inspire us to think tricky.

Just exactly how tricky this conspiratorial, electronic
world can be we demonstrated during the caper of the
Eighteen-Minute Buzz. That was the buzz on the Nixon
tapes that conveniently obliterated some very crucial
Oval-Office dialogue, which might have fatally damaged the
stonewalling president a lot sooner, had it been intelligible.
There was quite a dispute going on about whether the tapes
had been edited by Nixon, perhaps vacuum-cleaned by
Rose Mary Woods, or whether the President was simply the
pathetic victim of what his chief aide, General Haig, called
"some Sinister Force." Most audio experts at the time were
leaning toward the Haig version of random happenstance,
convinced that no tampering by presidential fingers could
fool them.
   What a challenge for *As It Happens*. Having covered
Watergate from the beginning, when you still had to explain
to most people — including their professional colleagues —
that Woodward and Bernstein were not a song-writing
team, here was our chance to go past mere reporting and
make ourselves a part of the Watergate scene.
   Our mad genius, Max Allen (later to become more famous for bringing on probably the largest libel claim in the
history of Commonwealth law with his documentary, "Dying of Lead"), placed want ads in dozens of newspapers in
Canada, the US, and Britain, inviting audio experts to challenge his doctored tapes. And then Max took his magic razor
blade and went to work on old Barbara Frum interviews —
turning yes's into no's, questions into answers, totally reversing meanings, defying his experts from around the world to
detect even one of them. They failed. And their failure was
news.

As It Happens had crashed Watergate. Sam Ervin called for *our* tapes to add to his Nixon collection. Editorialists used our results as a talking point against the terrible tools available to The Conspiracy. We even made ourselves a miniscule footnote in the Kennedy assassination story when beleaguered ex-New Orleans DA, Jim Garrison, called for our Watergate tapes as courtroom ammunition for his personal, on-going tilt with those Sinister Forces.

Three
Retailing Bliss

My father was a merchant, and a pretty successful one. He made his original stake in the twenties, selling fancy boots and silk shirts to the high-paid riggers and excavators who came to dig the Welland Canal. I don't remember it being deliberate, yet somehow he outfitted me, too. He taught me that you don't buy labels, you don't buy hype, and you always finger the merchandise. It's because of him that I am an anathema to the gurus, astrologers, palm readers, graphologists, bio-rhythm advocates, astral travellers, aura analysers, and all the others out there who peddle the life-changing message. Self-improvement is *the* product for the nervous 1970s, and the slicker the packaging, the closer I want to look.

With the show-biz psychic, Uri Geller, I was downright inhospitable. We had managed to get an interview with the Israeli charmer on his first trip to Canada, right after he'd dazzled the scientists at California's Stanford Research Institute with his "unexplainable" powers. Geller claims to bend metal by stroking it, to see drawings through sealed envelopes, and to describe the contents of ladies' handbags from 300 feet away. He did all those tricks for the scholars at Stanford and no one there could figure out how.

The people I work with were not only ready, they were hungry for such miracles. But, for network air time, they thought they deserved more from Geller than just a few bent keys and spoons in the Toronto studio. Here was a man, after all, who stood accused of causing an unwanted pregnancy by bending an IUD out of useful shape. Putting that kind of magnetism on radio would surely send clocks into seizure in all five time zones. Maybe it would even get us a lawsuit from an irate listener in Inuvik whose silverware had deformed at the seductive sound of Geller's voice

I don't mind admitting that I was tense. If Stanford research scientists with all their lab equipment had been unable to detect Geller's methods, vigilance alone was hardly much of a tool. One thing for sure, I was determined that I wouldn't make it easy for him. Nor was I moved by the pleas of my colleagues, who did not want to have to tell the country, "Tonight on *As It Happens*, Uri Geller does *not* bend a key."

As it turned out, that's exactly what happened. Under my baleful eye, alas, graphologists can't graph, astrolinks fail to connect, and Uri Geller does not bend anything. For twenty solid minutes he laboured over my keys – my car key, my house key (Geller likes to work on objects that have emotional significance), turning them, rubbing them, asking questions about them. Nothing. And in the control room I could see my heartsick colleagues pacing furiously, muttering, "Hey, man, dig Frum with the negative vibes," blaming *me* for the absence of miracles. I guess they had a point, because as soon as our session ended and Geller was able to escape from my presence into the friendliness of the control room, his psychic powers returned and, surrounded by admiring fans, Geller bent keys by the dozen.

Uri Geller's genius is that he is much more than just a clever stage magician. He is as serious a merchant of human potential as the gurus of Transcendental Meditation, Scientology, est, or Hare Krishna, but with this difference: Geller sells by example. Unlike the others who market systems, he makes his money by *not* telling you how to do it. If Geller convinces you that it is the mysterious, unknown power of his mind that's reshaping metal and communicating telepathically, then he is living proof of the hidden, untapped potential of the human brain. And if the bliss merchants are making their bank managers smile these days, it's because there are millions of people who desperately want to believe in their own untapped potential and who will gladly pay to have that faith confirmed.

A million North Americans now believe that the Maharishi Mahesh Yogi has the big answer. No amount of disillusioning news that meditation may be simply fancy cat-napping seems to hurt their guru's image, or his twelve-million-dollar-a-year enterprise. In the spring of 1975 the Maharishi came to Ottawa to launch the Age of Enlightenment for the whole world. While he was at it, he ran a private session for our Members of Parliament. A room full of ohm-chanting parliamentarians had to be taken seriously. And so we asked the Maharishi to our Ottawa studio. He came, but only after considerable arm-twisting. Transcendental Meditation's Ottawa friends feared that their guru wouldn't get the proper respect, although why they're so defensive about him I have no idea. The Maharishi can not only take care of himself, his marketing style makes K-Tel sound reticent. Notice how he manages to work in more mentions of his product in this five-minute interview than the CRTC allows normal advertisers in an hour of network time. Of course, he does it charmingly.

Hello, I am Barbara Frum.
    Very good.
How do you do?
    Beautiful. I inaugurated the dawn of the Age of Enlightenment for the whole of North America today, this morning, this being the first day of spring, 1975.
To what end, Maharishi, what are you after?
    Greater happiness. More hope for people. Less problems in society, more ideas in society — in Canada and all over North America.
And after you proclaim enlightenment, what do we all have to do to get there?

Fifteen minutes morning and evening, practise of Transcendental Meditation. That's all that is necessary.

Didn't you used to say thirty minutes? Have you trimmed back?

Oh, yes, because as more and more people are meditating, the environment is becoming more and more orderly, so we are reducing the time of meditation.

How deep a meditation does it have to be to work?

One just has to learn Transcendental Meditation and then it takes the awareness to a great depth, which then keeps the mind on a very orderly level of performance.

How many people do you think you have to get meditating before we've got an enlightened world?

One per cent of the world's population. That would show a very remarkable change from problems to solutions and harmony in the world.

I've got a quote of yours here, Maharishi, that I'd like you to comment on.

Yes?

You say life is bliss, not suffering.

That's right.

That certainly contradicts my experience.

This is because the education has been so inadequate. The full potential of life is infinite and boundless. Once one begins to meditate, the inner potentiality develops. Problems begin to fall away and more and more fulfilment is experienced. That is why we want to introduce the science of creative intelligence in all levels of education, so that man develops that ability to be spontaneously functioning in accordance with all the laws of nature.

I would have thought that if the mind became more clear, we would see the truth about life, which is not bliss —

Oh, truth is all bliss. That certain stage of the mind which we call "transcendental consciousness," this level is bliss consciousness, it's pure consciousness. It's the most orderly state of the mind.

But don't most human beings, Maharishi, run around, running to parties, making trouble, to kind of blur the mind, because they can't face what life really is, which is that we're all born to die and a few horrible truths like that?

Parties also are necessary. Running about is also necessary. But what is primarily needed is that certain state of the mind which one gets in fifteen minutes of morning and evening Transcendental Meditation. With this the mind becomes settled and then all these parties begin to be enjoyed much more than what they are now today.

How is that different from what Dale Carnegie spoke about years ago, or Coué in the twenties with his "Day by day, in every way, I am getting better and better"?

I don't know what Dale said but what I know about Transcendental Meditation is that those who use this procedure, fifteen minutes morning and evening, begin to enjoy life more, begin to progress more, and find fulfilment more and more. That is what results from my procedure. What is necessary is to have life lived on a natural level of freedom from problems.

Maharishi, what do you think about some of your competitors who have a similar message to yours? I'm thinking of the Maharaj Ji—people like that.

I invite all other systems to turn to Transcendental Meditation because this has proved very effective and is now giving rise to a beautiful world.

You don't like—

Why waste time in something that is not scientifically evident to be very right and all-comprehensively right? More efficient and more natural and more simple and more universal?

Less gobble-de-gook.

That's it.

Maharishi, it's been delightful to talk to you.

And all my love and great greetings to the whole population of Canada. Because we are inaugurating the Age of Enlightenment here, I am sure very soon the Canadian population will have 1 per cent and we'll have the sun shine for the whole world from this great nation of Canada.

Fantastic. Thank you very much.

It's beautiful.

How come you're so happy?

It's natural. It's the nature of life. Life is bliss.

I must remember that, Maharishi.

Life is bliss.
I must remember that.

In the Canadian tradition of fair play, a few words from the competition. Swami Vishnu Devananda, whose thing is yoga, says TM is not the real way. He spent twenty thousand dollars on a full-page ad in *Newsweek* Magazine to tell North Americans that they were being "hoodwinked" by the TM organization. The Tranquillity War was on. A steamed-up Swami Vishnu had to talk a mile a minute to get it all out.

What do you mean by "hoodwink," Swami Vishnu?
> Hoodwink means they're not telling the truth about mantra. They want to charge $125. That is against the rule. The Maharishi's yoga master did not charge $125 for initiating Maharishi.

Do you mind the charge? Or the lie that each mantra is a unique one?
> The lie is the most important thing. You see, they're afraid people will find out that they sell the same mantra to everybody.

This isn't just sour grapes on your part, is it?
> Pardon?

Do you know the expression "sour grapes"?
> Yes. I know sour grape. Oh, yes. If you want to tell me the sour grape, then I don't have to put the twenty-thousand-dollar ad and the rough words. It's not publicity for us. I am only trying to help American people and also the future yoga teachers coming into the West, so they won't be all told they're coming to make money.

Some people think that North Americans want everything too quickly.
> That's why they took LSD, to find the truth very fast, is it not?

I think so.
> One hundred and twenty-five dollars — look how cheap you are looking for things.

The Maharishi tells me I can have bliss if I just meditate fifteen minutes morning and evening.

Yes?

But you're going to tell me it's harder than that. Maybe you're not even going to offer me bliss.

For the fool's paradise it can be bliss. You know "fool's paradise"? That's what it is. Twenty minutes with a concocted mantra and you will be in fool's paradise. This kind of thing only can be sold in America. American people must be the most gullible people in the world.

It didn't take the bliss moguls long to discover the potential in the North American youth market. Maharaj Ji (who, after all, is just a kid himself), the Reverend Sun Myung Moon, and L. Ron Hubbard have made a fortune selling a sense of purpose and a reason to get up in the morning to middle-class kids who don't know what to do with their expendable dollars and their expendable lives. What the gurus market is joy. For that, they demand something that their purchasers don't value anyway, control of their lives.

When she was sixteen, Linda Epstein bought Hare Krishna. For three years she happily hit the pavement on Yonge Street in Toronto every day, begging-cup in hand, blissfully content to be a cipher in a sari. Linda collected money for a destination she didn't know or question. Like Scientology, the Divine Light Mission, or the brand of Christianity marketed by that Mao in a business suit, Sun Myung Moon, Hare Krishna works by keeping its followers ignorant of everything except the movement's particular brand of truth.

Linda Epstein was as unremarkable as all the other devotees and might have remained so, except for the fact that her father decided to tussle for her mind and hired Lightning Ted Patrick to restore her to her senses. Thanks to the cults, Patrick has his own little industry going, selling his de-programming services to hurt and angry parents who can't bear the embarrassing defection of their rebellious offspring. Patrick works on the theory that the cultists are brainwashed victims of sinister masterminds, victims who will only be saved when the trance is forcibly broken. It's a pleasing explanation, no doubt, to parents who don't understand how their children could knowingly reject them.

When Ted Patrick was finished de-programming Linda, a press conference was called to celebrate the family's re-union – as though the parents thought that some publicity would vindicate their pain and solidify their victory over Hare Krishna.

It didn't work. In a matter of weeks, Linda was back downtown at the temple. I've talked to her twice on *As It Happens*, once while she was grateful for being rescued from the cult and later when she was grateful to be back. On the first occasion, the "retrieved soul" sounded rather fran-tic. Her answers came back at me so fast and so jumbled that she was almost unintelligible.

Are you Linda?

Yes, I'm Linda, and I'd like to make a few points at the beginning. I'm not going back to the temple, whatever means they try. We only got like one meal a day and slept four hours. And we were working, selling books very hard on the street like for about six hours, seven hours, eight hours a day. It wasn't out of my own free will but because the pull of the hypnosis was so strong. I collected like maybe a hundred dollars a day on the street. I was so tired. I was really overworked. Sometimes I'd fall asleep on the street. And I'm really glad to be back because like I was just completely overworked.

What kept you then? Why didn't you walk out the door?

I was under the hypnosis and total brainwashing. I was afraid, psychologically afraid to leave, because if I left I would have nowhere to go because my mind was at-tracted to the chanting and I just had nowhere to go. My mind was programmed to think that I should just keep chanting and thinking I was doing the work for God.

Can you tell us how you were programmed?

Through continuous chanting of the Hare Krishna man-tra, like four hours in the morning, four hours in the evening, classes, scriptures, chanting, and they make you think that you're working for God and that every-thing should be given up for God. So they have people sent out on the streets to take money from people and –

But Linda, if you were so overworked and underfed, what kept you there? Do you remember wanting to get away and not being able to?

It's like when anyone's hypnotized, you're in a trance. Like I thought I was giving up for God. I was programmed to think that. We have no choice. Psychologically, we were afraid to leave. Sometimes people leave on their own, but they have nowhere to go. They just don't know where they're going to work. They just don't fit into society. So Ted Patrick, he's the de-programmer, he takes people out by permission of their parents and he tells you the evils of the cult. There's different cults. There's five hundred of them. And he tells you how you're being tricked, how you're being used as a prostitute.

That's what Ted Patrick said?

He says that to everyone. He says the same amount of words to everyone during the de-programming.

The next time I saw Linda was in the studio several months later, right after she went back to Hare Krishna — just as giddy, just as frenzied, just as convinced now that she was right in rejecting her father and Ted Patrick — but clearly a lot more contented.

Why did you go back, Linda?

Why? Because I was pulled out against my own will and I had a repressed desire in me to go back all the time, but my father said that if I went back he'd personally grab me and then they'd have the de-programmers for four months and they'd keep me in a room. I was really scared because I was really confused. They were shooting down everything I've ever done and they were blaspheming our movement and our spiritual master and I was just so scared, I didn't know what to do. I'd see the devotees downtown. I'd talk to them. How can you ignore them? I've known them for years. They're my friends and the only people I really care for. I just want to know God and this is my way of doing it, you know. My father is an atheist and if he doesn't want to do it, it's fine with me.

What do you mean by saying that the devotees are the only people in the world you care about? Your father and mother cared enough to want to save you from making a terrible mistake and from being controlled.

I'm not controlled. I can come and go freely and see my parents if I want. No one forced me to come back. I came back on my own. Like when they pulled me out, they gave me a list of things to say and my father said he'd beat the hell out of me if I didn't say them.

We talked to you then, too, and you were just as convinced that Hare Krishna had brainwashed you. Which is it? Which is really you?

See, the thing is, like Ted Patrick has a philosophy — this brainwashing philosophy — that people are hypnotized and this and that. I never heard about that until he started talking to me. And like he completely breaks your resistance down. I didn't know what to think and I started accepting what he was thinking because that's the only thing that I kept hearing over and over again and I was just so scared.

Yet when you were describing the de-programming, you said you were scared at first, but then you realized that Ted Patrick cared about you and about helping you.

But every day I could tell that I was missing them. I would talk about the devotees and Krishna and the temple and I kept thinking about going back, but I didn't have enough courage, because I was threatened that if I went back — like there's a Hell's Angel who's a de-programmer and I didn't want to do that whole thing again, that whole torture thing, with all this yelling and screaming and Bible verses and all these things. Like, I'm not kidding, they'd make a list of things I'd have to say and if I didn't say them, my father said they'd beat the hell out of me.

What's the state of relations between you and your parents? Are you going to be able to talk to them ever again?

I hope so. They don't really want to talk to me. I called them twice in the last two months.

What did they say?

"We don't want to talk to you or have anything to do with

you. Don't bother us. Why don't you just come home?"

Do you feel for them at all?

Yeah, because they don't try to understand. They can't
live my life forever, you know.

What do you think brought you back to the temple?

Chanting Hare Krishna and the devotees. The girls there
that I knew.

Is it a special caring that you got from them?

Well, yeah, we're all endeavouring to become God-
conscious, to become Krishna-conscious together.

Then again, your parents also love you. They gave birth to
you and reared you.

Yeah, but we try to not be attached. I was never really
getting love. I never really was close to them, anyways. I
don't miss them now or anything. I never missed them
before, either. I call them every now and then and just
keep a distant relationship. A lot of people do that
because there's nothing there. Like, I thought maybe if I
went back to school and contacted old friends, I'd be
happy, but I wasn't happy. I just kept getting back to
Krishna-conscious activities. So the proof is there. Like,
I wasn't really de-programmed — whatever that means.
It's obvious that my father didn't get his money's worth.

What do you see ahead for Linda Epstein?

Becoming God-conscious. Like, I've always been interested in finding out about God. I'm here and I enjoy
what I'm doing — telling people about Krishna and selling
books and things. You know.

The seventies have been boom times for products with
an Eastern motif. I was momentarily into Chinese bangs and
a quilted jacket myself. Kung Fu and Karate studios are
thriving, jade decorates the most fashionable necks, and
acupuncture "cures" everything from migraine to tennis
elbow.

I don't know for sure that acupuncture doesn't work. But
the people who swear by it can't show how it does. For me,
that takes acupuncture out of science into cultism. Sometimes I get the feeling that Western converts have more faith

in the silver needles than do the Chinese themselves. It seems that my cynicism is shared by David Quastel, who is an Associate Professor of Pharmacology at the University of British Columbia. He ought to know.

Professor Quastel, why are you so skeptical about acupuncture if you've never seen it?
> Mainly because it turns out, from the description of some Canadian doctors with the investigating team visiting China, that in these surgical operations done with the patient awake, and said to be anaesthetised with acupuncture, we now find out that these patients have been given sedatives. They've been given conventional narcotic analgesics – that's pain killers. We find also that they have been trained beforehand in breathing exercises and relaxing exercises. They've been selected for high pain thresholds. It's only very few operations which are done in this way. And there isn't much pain associated with them in the first place.

And yet, every team that's gone to China and has seen acupuncture in action comes back with glowing reports of brain tumours removed, skulls opened.
> Ah, yes. Well, first of all, it seems that they don't mind using a local anaesthetic if the patient complains of a little pain. And brain operations are notoriously pain-free. There's no pain associated with cutting into the brain's surface. I'll give you a quote from Samuel Johnson: "Questioning is not the mode of conversation among gentlemen." Well, the people we send to China are gentlemen. They're guests of the Chinese Republic and they act in the proper gentlemanly fashion.

But surely the Chinese aren't putting on an act. After all, they're using their own people for this purpose. And when a person is asked, under acupuncture, in surgery, "How do you feel?" and he says, "Okay," he surely wouldn't lie. You can't brainwash people for 5,000 years.
> Look, the question for us is, how useful is this modification of pain in practice?

What about the films we've seen of stomach operations using acupuncture?

> It turns out that they don't really do much abdominal
> operation with acupuncture. The muscle relaxation is
> terrible, so it's terribly hard work for the surgeon. And
> I'm not sure that it really helps the patient to be awake
> during the operation.

Is this an emperor's clothes situation, then? Because we've
sent dozens of Canadian doctors to China and they all come
home rapturous.

> Well, what are they supposed to do, insult their hosts?
> But they could be skeptical. I mean, doctors are notorious
> for putting down new ideas.

> You know, the point is this. There's a need for a lot of
> research in pain. There's a need for a lot of research in
> anaesthesia. But the Canadian government doesn't want
> to pay for research. They figure they can let the Ameri-
> cans do it; we can import it. I think there's a lot of that in
> acupuncture. Are we to go to China and emerge with
> nothing? No. So we go to China and, in the good free-
> loading tradition, we bring back acupuncture. I don't
> think that the politicians' delight in Chinese food in
> Peking is sufficient reason for distorting the whole medi-
> cal research program into what's convenient politically.
> And I'm not sure that there's much more to acupuncture
> than that.

It's not hard to understand why Yankee *entrepreneurs*
would be offended that Eastern imports were getting an
unfair share of the bliss business. After all, there are tens of
millions of dollars in hard currency up for grabs here. So,
just as the Pacer was put forward in answer to Toyota,
Western inventions like Re-birthing and est and rolfing
were sent forth to compete for the nirvana dollar.

Re-birthing is one of the newer human-potential games
for grown-ups. It's for those people who are ready to go past
material striving onto "the self's potential to know and to
be." But this is the bonus — Re-birthing assures its custom-
ers that in the next round they'll be walking like Gods on
Earth. I thought the technique sounded a little dangerous,
but it only takes an hour and there's at least the satisfaction of

working at your potential for greatness – which puts you way ahead of the unenlightened masses who don't have the courage to even try. Freelance journalist Jesse Kornbluth tried Re-birthing for us.

Mr. Kornbluth, why would somebody want to be Re-birthed?

> The basic idea of this is that there is no reason for any of us to die. As Leonard Orr, the founder of the Re-birthing technique says, "Death is a grave mistake."

True.

> So what you must do is clean up the very first moment of your life, because you were born in a hostile environment. You were slapped. You were forced to breathe right away through your lungs, and that is such a negative experience that it colours everything that happens to you for the rest of your life. It makes you feel that life does not love you. The purpose of the Re-birth experience is to clean up that garbage so that you can see that life loves you and that you are a God upon this Earth, and that everything is really designed for your use.

How does any of that help us avoid death?

> Well, what you must do is write daily a series of things called "affirmations." What you do is simply say, "I am a healthy being. I deserve to live forever. I am beautiful and wonderful." And you write that a number of times each day until it becomes a part of your consciousness. In so doing, Mr. Orr holds, you may possibly live forever.

What does the charismatic Mr. Orr offer you at your Re-birth?

> Actually, Orr is unusual in that he is deliberately non-charismatic. He's very low-keyed. He simply says he's found a way and invites you to try it out, too. What actually happens at the Re-birth is that you get into a large redwood tub naked, with water heated to about 101 degrees. You then put a snorkel into your mouth, nose-clips over your nose, and you lie face down, floating in this water.

Who's there with you?

> I was Re-birthed by a sex therapist and her boyfriend.

What was the other guy doing there? Protecting her or offering alternatives?

> They simply serve to lift you out of the tub and assure you that you're in a safe psychological space. They put you on a towelled table until you have recovered, or "experienced-out," as they say, your birth trauma. You see, there is a critical point at which the heat of the water gets to you. You seem to be paralysed or palsied. What you're doing, of course, is hyper-ventilating, which has nothing to do with birth, but has a lot to do with being in a tubful of hot water.

How many people can they handle per day in this water bath?

> They do about three or four people a day. And they have Re-birthed about 5,000 people at fifty dollars a head in the last year and a half. That makes it a very rapidly growing business in the consciousness field.

So Mr. Orr is making money at this?

> Mr. Orr is not only making money, he is delighted to be making money. This is what distinguishes him from other gurus, who pretend that they're not. Orr believes that it is his destiny to be rich, and if you bring somebody to be Re-birthed he'll give you 10 per cent of the fee. Another interesting consciousness-raiser Orr runs is a money seminar, where you pay Mr. Orr 10 per cent of your monthly income, and come once a month and talk about money. He believes that simply by focusing your attention on money, and by being willing to give money to someone who doesn't need it, it frees up your own feelings about money and enables you to make much more of it. He believes we're all on Earth to get rich and live forever.

If you didn't find the answer in Re-birthing, Primal Therapy, or the "What is/is" message of est-founder Werner Erhard, TM, TA, Creative Dreaming, or *The Joy of Sex*, there's still HIM — not Him — but Human Individual Metamorphosis, led by the outer-space team of Bo and Peep. You're laughing? Me, too. The news that dozens of people on the west coast were suddenly leaving home and possessions, kids and jobs, to go into the desert with their life savings and wait for a flying saucer to come and lift them to the next kingdom — well, it had to be a hoax, a put-on of every mystical cult that ever promised heaven on Earth. Nobody was nervy enough — even in this kook-tolerant time — to go out in broad daylight and propose such a thing. And if they tried, surely nobody would ever buy it.

Wrong, wrong. Joan Culpepper was one of many who bought this west-coast novelty and she's spent forty summers on this planet, which usually means something. Culpepper joined The Two, Bo and Peep, in April of 1975. She wandered with them for three long months before the charismatic duo decided that she was too strong-willed to go to the next world.

When and where did you first meet this couple claiming to be from outer space, Miss Culpepper?

> I met them at a meeting that was held in my home in Hollywood. This was in April. I met them through a very respected metaphysical teacher in the area, who called me to tell me that he had met them. He thought they were enlightened people and that I would be interested in calling a group of people together for a meeting.

We've heard many reports of Bo and Peep and their mesmerizing hold on people. What was your reaction to them?

> Rather than mesmerize, I would say it was more like mind control. Mesmerizing takes a period of time to re-program you, as it were. These two people had the ability to, in a matter of minutes, get into your head and implant ideas. So to me this wasn't hypnotism but mental control.

What kind of a trip did they lay out? Was it, "Leave your house behind, leave your family, leave your money" from the beginning?

> That's true. Well, not leave your money. We were told to sell everything we could sell and bring as much money with us as possible, because we would need it. But, yes, from the very beginning, the whole trip was, you know, leave everything behind that you're attached to at the human level, and this includes your children.

And where were you going? Was a space trip on a UFO there right from the beginning?

No. The UFO came into play only in August. Initially, these two people claimed only that they were going to be killed, that they would resurrect after three and a half days in the same way that Jesus Christ did, and that they and their followers would then be lifted off of the planet in a beam of light.

Oh—

A beam of light would appear to the Earthlings, as they call us. It would appear to be a UFO, but it was not a UFO. The UFO story got started in August because, as one of the girls who stayed with them told me when the story broke, "We have changed our entire approach." In fact, her words to me were, "We're going to hit hard and heavy on the UFO, because that's what the public is interested in. It's the only way we can get any publicity for Bo and Peep."

Was it only a money rip-off or was it truly a spiritual group?

I do not feel that it was a con-game in the normal sense of the word. They do take your money if you have any with you. From our group they collected between thirteen thousand and thirty-five thousand dollars. That was from twenty people. But that's gravy. The real rip-off, in my opinion, comes because they're ripping off people's minds.

Was any of it a good experience?

It was horrible. I spent a lot of time crying, a lot of time feeling very despondent, very despairing and fearful. They kept us so busy that we didn't have time to think. This was one of the methods they used to brainwash you. They instilled fear patterns. They instilled isolation patterns.

What do you mean?

They claimed that if you made contact with anyone you had left behind that the spirit entities in another plane of existence — who were against Bo and Peep in making this trip — would maim or kill those that you had left behind. They isolated us, stripped us of our identities. We were not allowed to use our real names. We weren't even encouraged to talk to anybody else in the campsite outside of the group.

So this was not exactly an orgiastic group?

Absolutely not. Sex was out. Smoking was out. Everything was out. You could do nothing but listen to these
two people, do everything that they said, and do nothing
that they considered human. And I don't like to admit it,
but I have been a little up-tight that I have been the only
one who's come back and been willing to talk about it.
Sounds like you're still afraid of them.
I think anyone is dangerous who has the ability to control others mentally.

Four
Sociology for Fun and Profit

Thank goodness for sociology – it fills in so many of the blanks. It tells you that people in elevators get squirmy if you stare at them, that ugly people make more grateful marriage partners, that short people aren't as tall as tall people, that Italians and Jews are inclined to holler when they're in pain, and that people read in the bathroom to kid themselves about what they're doing there. Were tax dollars not paying for it, I don't think I'd mind so much. If sociologists find it stimulating to observe the obvious and the useless, who am I to quibble?

But when a social scientist can talk government out of a third of a million dollars, in this period of restraint, so he can show dirty movies to college students who are high on marijuana while he monitors their enjoyment level on their wired-up private parts – well, I'm annoyed. Especially when I'd have been glad to tell him the answer for $1.25 – no wires, no waterpipe – and I've never been high on marijuana in my life. You should have heard how sore he got when I wanted to know what possible good the answers would ever do anybody when he had them.

I had another sociologist upset with me. This one was working the well-tilled ground of prostitution theory. I suggested that her findings hardly warranted her methods.

Miss Stein, where did you actually park yourself?
　　It depended on the apartment – behind the drapes, behind the door. Some girls had peep holes in their apartments set up for their exhibitionistic or voyeuristic clients.
Didn't you feel shabby?
　　Didn't I feel what?
Shabby. I mean, the guy's paid good money for privacy.
　　I don't think they were paying for privacy. They were paying for their sessions. No, I didn't feel shabby. I mean, does any other type of researcher feel shabby when they are observing some element of human behaviour?

Maybe I was a little hard on Miss Stein and her "Lovers, Friends and Slaves" study. But she really rattled my civil-libertarian cage with her "scientific" peeping. I'm much more tolerant when it's only rats they're watching. The researcher who was looking into urban rodent stress – sending his laboratory rats through morning and evening rush hour every day for fifteen years, now, by playing tapes of subway noises to them while he mechanically vibrates their cages – that guy got a very sympathetic hearing from me.

I also adore those human-behaviour studies that only want to be entertaining. Don't we all feel better to have it verified in the laboratory that big-breasted women have tiny brains, that emotional depression is good for us, and that tall men with full heads of hair *don't* have better sex lives? Results like that make me much more kindly disposed toward all the sociologists, psychologists, and behaviourists – the benefactors *and* the entertainers – who toil in the vineyards of human behaviour and only want to understand.

You've got to feel for Dr. Edwin Shneidman of UCLA. All he tried to do was find out why some people decide to kill themselves. It seemed to him a study of their suicide notes might turn up some useful clues. How depressing for him to learn that people who jump off buildings aren't at their analytical best in their final moments. Nor are they long-winded. Last messages tend to contain little more information than: "Dear Harold, Goodby, I'm sorry."

Dr. Shneidman, what does a typical suicide note say?

Oh, it says, "Please forgive me"; or, "I'm sorry to have to do this"; or, "Take care of the automobile." You get notes like: "Change the spark plugs on our car, I'm about to end my life" — which is banal. It's obvious that he's about to end his life. Or someone who says, "I've lost the road," and so on.

How do professional writers do on their suicide notes? Did Hemingway, for example, leave anything behind?

No, but Virginia Woolf left a note addressed to her husband, which said, in effect, that she was going mad again. She was falling into another depression, but she didn't want to burden him with this; he must go on doing his own writing. She asked for his understanding and his forgiveness. She then drowned herself, as you know. Now that's really not — for a person who is as lucid and articulate and as profoundly introspective as Virginia Woolf was — a terribly profound note.

I wonder if you're not being too picky here. Surely Leonard knew why. And she was only writing to him, after all, not to us or to some psychiatric board.

But the note is redundant. Let's say, for example, someone hangs herself and the husband then comes home and sees her body hanging. Seeing the hanging body tells you, really, all you need to know. A suicide note is probably one of the most redundant of all human documents.

Is it maybe just a tradition? Something you're supposed to do, like sending Christmas cards?

No — gee whiz, that's a breathtaking analogy. No, I'm convinced that the people who write the notes think that they're communicating much more than the words say.

For all their disappointments and shortcomings, sociologists do often provide a very useful human service. They've made it respectable to wonder out loud about things we'd otherwise be ashamed to be thinking about. Thanks to them, we now know, for example, that men with pendulous earlobes turn women on; that Paul Newman is a sex object because the paleness of his cornea allows movie fans to follow the dilations and contractions of his pupils; that our sleeping positions reveal our personalities (on the back – open; on the side and curled up – closed); and that gynecologists seduce their patients more frequently than do doctors of any other branch.

By now it must be as hard to come up with a fresh PHD topic in the social sciences as it is to find a labour leader who's for wage and price controls. You can appreciate, therefore, how startled I was to learn that an entire erogenous zone had just been discovered by an investigator in New York City. The armpit, according to Benjamin Brody, is a most important part of our sexual equipment and should never be sprayed or shaven. And if you need his credentials before you'll accept a concept like that, Dr. Brody is on the faculties of the William Alanson White Institute of Psychiatry and Adelphi University in New York.

You've done an awful lot of work on armpits, Dr. Brody.

Yes. I'm not the first, incidentally. Havelock Ellis, who was one of the great pioneers in the whole study of sex, was very interested in the *axillae* – that's the scientific word for armpits – and I got some of my good cases from him.

Some of your ideas about the armpit make me fear we're going to offend some people.

I hope not. We'll try to be as antiseptic and clinical as possible.

But antiseptic armpits aren't what the doctor ordered, I understand.

No, but that's been the tendency in contemporary society. We have relegated sexually permissive zones to one or two areas. The others have been ignored or wiped away. Now, it's my conviction – not only mine, but that of many other scientists – that practically every surface area of the body can be sexually useful, even pleasureful.

But why has the armpit got such significance to you?

First of all because, like the female genitals, they are apertures, more or less hidden away, covered with coarse hair. They produce a secretion, they produce an odour. And the secretions and the odours are intimately related to the secretions and the odours of the genitals.
What kind of case studies have you looked at?

I was seeing an attractive young woman who'd been quite promiscuous in her desperation and I was struck by her seductiveness from the very beginning of my work with her. She, of course, denied this. One day she lifted her hands to her hair. That's a classic female gesture isn't it? She calls attention to her hair, but at the same time, the armpit is exposed.
It also raises the breast, Doctor.

It also raises the breast.
You may be confused here.

No, I think both of these things are operating. She did this when she was wearing a sleeveless dress. And then she said to me, "I see it all. I'm asking you to come on. I'm showing you the secret hairy part." In that moment she realized that she was being seductive.
Do women get turned on by men's armpits, too?

Women, unfortunately, are not liable to admit such a thing. But there is no question that human beings in general can be attracted by the other person's odour. An important part of that is armpit odour.
Doctor, I'll give you one clue that you may want to follow up. Women like basketball players.

Aha – Okay. Many, many instances of that. Many, many instances of that.
And you have to lift your arm if you're going to get the ball in the basket.

Lately, it seems, there are more people analysing sex than doing it. As a result, the remotest areas of the sexual landscape are being reconnoitred by the scouts from the social sciences. Robert Levin, for example, thought he'd look into the sex lives of women who go to church a lot. He discovered they not only had better marriages, they were also more sexually content.

How do you account for the results of your study, Mr. Levin?

> Partly, I think that it's because women who are strongly religious are probably more likely to be positive people in life. They are also more likely to accept limitations in life without questioning. They have a degree of acceptance, if you will, of life with all it's pluses and minuses.

But your results don't suggest that they're satisfied with less. Your results suggest they're getting more.

> They're not getting more. They have the same frequency of intercourse as the non-religious women. It's just that the strongly religious woman is more likely to be satisfied with her frequency than is the non-religious woman.

Isn't that interesting.

> But it also fits. When you accept, as religious people do, that life requires something of you — that it's not all taking, there's a degree of giving that's necessary — I think that plays an important part in sexual behaviour, especially in marriage.

But how do you account for these women being more orgasmic?

> I think we can account for that in this way. Religious groups now are emphasizing the desirability of sexual satisfaction in marriage, so we shouldn't be surprised if strongly religious women take these admonitions seriously. Therefore, the fact that she is more orgasmic doesn't come as a surprise to me.

Then again, could it be that religious wives are more contented because they tend to have religious husbands who stay at home?

> Well, it might be an important part of it, might it not? That's a reasonable hypothesis. Also, I suspect that when you're religious you have a strong sense of marriage being permanent. Now again, that is only a suspicion.

Is your wife religious, Mr. Levin?

> No, she is not.

That's a shame.

I'm not comfortable with Dr. Alex Comfort. I find his proselytizing on behalf of love and freedom not provocative but provoking. For me, sexual jealousy has always seemed a venerable and sensible institution. I liked Comfort better when he was still a gerontologist, travelling the circuit saying joyful things about growing old. Now that he's pushing the techniques of living better sensually, his broadmindedness and tolerance strike me as somewhat self-indulgent and hedonistic.

Dr. Comfort, do you think of monogamy as a prison that we are now escaping?

Well, it could be for some people, but for others it's not. I think the interesting thing now is that we're suffering from a lack of kin. Quite a lot of the swinging that goes on is done for the same reason the Eskimos do it, with a view to increasing the number of your nominal kin by advertising your friendships.

Sex to make buddies.

Yes, but it goes a bit farther because there's very intense bonding between people who share like that. We assume that they ought to be jealous of each other and get mad at each other, but people who do it don't in fact find that to be the case. Guys who share a woman tend to behave the way that apes and monkeys who share a partner do. There's a "David and Jonathan" thing between them. And instead of reacting the way society says they ought to react — I mean, rather like a backward five-year-old if he sees somebody else with his tricycle — they tend to become firm friends.

Are we all that flexible?

It seems that we can be any kind of "ogamous" that the times dictate. Humans have been polyandrous, they've been polygamous, they've been monogamous. Right now the social override is getting less important, so people are able to choose which lifestyle they personally can best adjust to. I would feel we're almost infinitely various. The change is not that we're abandoning monogamy or adopting polygamy, but that we're now coming to realize this variety.

And yet, look at someone as supposedly liberated as Simone De Beauvoir. This is a hunch I've had for a long time. She's made freedom an issue in her life — no children, no marriage — and yet she's said that if Sartre died she wondered what she would do. Perhaps she would commit suicide. That suggests to me something more powerful's at work here than just the intellect.

Oh, I think so. I think a primary relationship of that kind is absolutely vital to humans. Nobody's speaking against that. We all need some kind of stability. We all need one or more important primary relationships.

But why must those other relationships also be sexual?

They need not be. It depends on the person and the circumstances. There should be no compulsion on everybody to embark on a whole lot of secondary relationships if they don't wish. On the other hand, they shouldn't act as jailors to each other — what my wife rather nicely calls "penile servitude" for life, where the couple owns each other. Marriage was always a matter of kinship and property, right up to the Romantic movement, when it became a matter of keeping the courtship experience going throughout life. The property thing moved over into the idea of people owning each other. Quite a lot of people wouldn't necessarily choose the same person to live with as they choose to sleep with.

Doesn't that strike you as strange?

Why? Sex can be of three types, it can be reproductive, and it can express commitment, and it can be recreational. That's sex for babies, sex for love, and sex for fun. Some people know the lovely Irish story of the woman who kept having illegitimate babies until the Mother Superior said, "If you come into the hospital pregnant one more time, we won't have you here. Who is the man?" The woman answered, "It's Paddy Murphy." "He's not married, why do you not marry him?" "Because," she said, "I don't like him at all." It can happen.

Whatever it is you do, chances are some sociologist somewhere has already figured out why you do it. That's inevitable, I suppose, considering the ratio of inventive people (very few) to sociologists (very many). Bury yourself alive with snakes, eat butterflies, swim the channel, and Dr. Neil Smelser of Berkeley has your motives catalogued already in his files. I talked to him while Evel Knievel was hyping millions around the world into caring whether or not he'd make it across a canyon in Colorado in a rocket contraption. I couldn't have cared less about the stunt, or Knievel, but it sure puzzled me that so many of the people I cared about did. Could it be that in our bad times, as in the thirties, people need distractions like marathons and death-defying stunts?

Do you think that we do sillier things when the world is about to go down, Dr. Smelser?
    There is a sense of the absurd about a lot of the phenomena that pass in front of our eyes nowadays. Not just streaking and the daredevil kinds of activities – the return of the college prank culture. The collective conscience seems to be turning in this direction of absurdity at the moment, following a rather long period of quite serious expressions of concern over important matters.
What does the Evel Knievel business mean, for example?
    Well, it has a number of dimensions. One that is less appreciated than it might be is the religious overtones. If you examine it, it deals with all the fundamental issues that people have always built into their religions. You have the whole problem of destiny and mastering fate, the notion of luck and leading a charmed existence. There's a re-creation of the Valley of Death that is clearly religious in character. You have the whole notion of greed, of human appetite, and of contrition for that. The play on the word "evil" also conjures up dark forces at work. I have a feeling that one of the additional meanings of the Knievel business is clearly economic. It's the get-rich-quick, big gamble that has long been in the folklore of capitalism, associated with the stock market.
    It's beating the system big, in the face of uncertainty.
That certainly fits in with one thing that I've noticed, and that's that people who complain about being ripped off by inflation don't seem to mind being ripped off by Evel Knievel.

I think they identify with him, with the fact that he could get away with it, and thereby deal with feelings they have about being cheated themselves and hornswaggled by the inflationary erosions.

At least he could do it – he did it for them.

And he got away with it, that's right. While many people think of Knievel as a fraud, a snake, and a cheat, they sort of like the guy at one level and wish they could get away with the same thing.

We've got a particular situation in Canada that's interesting to us. An awful lot of teenagers, very unprepared teenagers, are trying to swim Lake Ontario. One young man has even lost his life trying it.

I think that for a thoroughly unprepared teenager to undertake that kind of thing – one hesitates to assign any kind of pathology to it – but one would have to look deeply for conflicts over exhibitionism, deep kinds of insecurity, feelings of worthlessness, and perhaps feelings of having been rejected. Quite clearly, here is an extraordinary bid for some kind of instant public notice and acclaim and affection, if you will.

Does it have to be cloaked in such negatives? Don't we all want to play roles? Don't we all want to be stars?

Of course. We all have those feelings. That's one reason why the efforts of these young people appeal to us.

They're such meaningless acts though, aren't they? A lake swim or marathon dancing or kissing contests or swallowing frogs or grasshoppers or spaghetti. We cover them all on this program and, believe me, it's easy. We could have one a night if we wanted.

But isn't there an element of meaning? In one way there is a denial of accomplishment by doing something silly. It's basically absurd. But by making a silly effort of this sort, you are almost apologizing for the serious intent, the exhibitionistic intent, that underlies it, because in the end you're really just a very silly, little person doing a silly, little thing, even though you're doing the most and the biggest and the best of it.

Of course, I don't dismiss all social science as frivolous. I'm really very enthusiastic about research that has some practical purpose. I've talked to many social scientists whose work directly and immediately benefits us all. Dr. Harvey Schlossberg, New York psychologist and police consultant, for example, has developed techniques that are now used all over the world to turn hostages into survivors. And now that being taken hostage has become one of the risks of living, I find that comforting to know.

How do you account for your success rate in talking down terrorists holding hostages, Dr. Schlossberg?

> I think what accounts for the success is that we look at the situation, not so much as a criminal act, but as a problem-solving situation — they're trying to tell us, "Hey, look, I've had it. I can't adjust. I can't accomplish. Help me." And we say, "We'd like to talk to you. We understand you're having difficulties. Can we help you?" And if they say "No," we'll wait — there's no particular rush.

How many different approaches are your negotiators trained to use?

> The negotiator plays whatever role he's cast into. It's not that he says, "Hey, today I'll be your father." He assumes whatever role the criminal casts him into.

Is the negotiator always physically safe?

> Like anything else, it has its risks. But as a rule we've found that, when people say they will accept you as a negotiator, they usually respect that. Even people with severe psychiatric problems. I guess it's part of our heritage. When somebody waves the white flag, we won't shoot him. That's kind of built-in.

What about all the cases we've had where the terrorists say they're going to shoot one person an hour?

> Yeah, but they don't.

But can you gamble that they won't?

> Well, we've been doing it. I would say that's almost universal. They will threaten, you know, if we don't get our demands, every half hour we'll throw out a body. Fortunately — and I knock on wood — not one has ever kept that promise.

One of the things that fascinates me, too, is the way some hostages will be released as the days go on. Sometimes it's a child. Sometimes it's a woman. What is in the terrorist's mind when he does that?

It's a barter kind of thing. You get partial releases in exchange for things. You know, you'd like cigarettes? Well, we'll give you cigarettes. Can you release one person. Or are you hungry? We'll trade food for one person. Occasionally they will spontaneously release hostages because they get too emotionally involved, like with a woman or with a child.

And that's fouling up their act?

Exactly.

Because they're sexually interested in the woman?

Well, not so much sexually interested. More because of our idea about mother and chivalry. They can't act out – or they feel artificial acting out – in front of mother. People make this mistake with suicides too. You know, maybe we should bring this guy's wife or his mother or his priest down to the scene.

What's wrong with that?

Well, this is the audience he's playing for. If this guy thought his mother loved him, he wouldn't be jumping.

But if the terrorist could scare his wife or his mother and really give them a lot of pain, mightn't that satisfy him?

Yeah. But what if he decides to scare them by killing somebody? Like, look what you've made me do.

Could we talk a bit about this incredible bond that seems to form between the terrorist and his hostage? The Ethiopian terrorists, for example. We talked to one of the men when he was released and he'd actually formed an emotional attachment to one of his captors. And this is not unusual, is it?

No. In fact, this is what our negotiating system works on, because the same kind of bond forms between the negotiator and the terrorist.

But here you are with a person who says he will kill you. How can you love a person like that?

It's much easier than you think. Here's this man who has life-and-death power over you and he's not killing you. He's a wonderful person.

But why is that sexually attractive? Remember the Swedish

bank-vault case?

That's right.

She came out and said she was going to marry the guy.

It's the potency. This man is almost God. He has life-and-death power. Look at all this power he's wielding and he's not hurting me. He's wonderful. The fact that he put her into that spot is really irrelevant.

You said that negotiators get into a relationship, too. What happens there? Do you start feeling guilty that you suckered him? Do you end up not wanting to trot him off to the pen?

Sure, we've had cases like that. It's the feeling that this guy had a point in what he was doing. You develop good feelings about the person, an understanding. You feel sorry for him. You can see his problem. You feel reluctant to arrest him. We've had cases like that. Of course, we go through with it.

What would you have done at Munich? That seems to remain the ultimate example of this kind of thing, doesn't it?

My feeling is that we would have kept them where they were and attempted to work out some sort of situation where they felt very good, in terms of making us look stupid, so they'd think, "Hey, we have enough power, let's go home and forget about it." I sure wouldn't have moved them around.

Are you prepared to lose? Get your hostages but lose the guy, and let him win his point?

Sure.

You've got no face on the line?

No. Our feeling is that human life is the most important thing because the cards are all in his hand as far as the hostages' lives are concerned. The primary aim is to save lives. We like him alive, too, if we can get him, but the hostages are our prime consideration. That's what we don't want to lose.

Schlossberg's kind of sociology nobody should make fun of. If you've seen the movie *Dog Day Afternoon* or followed recent hostage-taking dramas orchestrated by terrorists from Ireland or South Molucca or Mexico, you know how life-saving the findings of some social scientists can be.

Five
Surviving

In October, 1972, a party of young Uruguayan rugby players crashed in the frozen peaks of the Andes while flying to a match in Chile. They were lost for seventy days, until two of the hardiest and bravest managed to climb out of those desolate mountains and led rescuers to their helpless comrades. A year later the two young heroes were in North America to publicize the book *Alive*, which told their story. The book was a best-seller, not just because it described an extraordinary adventure, but because it vividly spelled out how the boys had refused to die of starvation and survived by eating the flesh of those who had been killed on impact. There were many people at the time who condemned the survivors, suggesting that cannibalism was too terrible an act to be condoned – which struck me as pretty pious. It was like saying that the boys should have died there, so that we could have praised them for their nobility. For me, the fact of cannibalism was only a distracting – although admittedly bizarre – detail, really only a symbol of what human beings are prepared to do to live.

When Nando Parrado and Roberto Canessa became available for interview, I decided to down-play the obvious and ghoulish aspects. Instead, I thought I'd concentrate on the psychological choices of staying alive, and on what they'd learned on that mountain about themselves and others. All had not been generosity and self-sacrifice among the Andes survivors; in fact, their survival had involved some pretty selfish and unheroic things. I wanted to hear about those aspects and about the kind of character it takes to keep on going in a seemingly hopeless situation.

Unfortunately, I got to talk to Parrado and Canessa only after they had become veterans of the talk-show circuit and had learned how to handle interviewers. As they came bustling into our New York studio, I could overhear them on the line—friendly, vital, easy-going young men, clearly enjoying the attention they were getting. About fifteen minutes into the interview, after it became obvious that the boys had turned the drama of their suffering into a pat performance, I hesitantly asked, "Would you be offended if I wondered if finally a human being doesn't have to be a bit of a bastard to survive a terrible event — if maybe saints don't make it?" Before I could establish whether they had understood what I was getting at, Canessa responded in the same humble, earnest manner he'd used in answering all my other questions.

"No. I think you must be a warm man to survive, because although I was suffering, if I'd died there, I would have felt that I'd tried my best for everybody."

It was a sweet answer but it didn't explain how people survive any better than had the rest of our conversation; although it struck me as interesting that it was Canessa, the domineering and difficult one on the mountain, who had answered, rather than Parrado, who was described as spoiled and thoughtless before the tragedy, but in crisis came as close as a human being can to selflessness.

Anyway, I let the subject drop and, after a few more exchanges, I said, "I wish you both good luck," to signal that I was about to sign off the line. Canessa, however, wasn't finished with me. The moment he thought we were off the air he jumped in hard.

"Do you still think we are bastards?" he demanded.

"I am sorry, Mr. Canessa," I answered uneasily. "You see, that's the trouble. What right have I got to stand in judgment of you? It's just that we all identify so much with you and what you've suffered. And we feel tormented because we fear that we would be no good at all."

"You feel that way?" he repeated, unsatisfied. And again I tried to explain what I had meant.

"You see, we're struggling to understand how a human being could have the strength to put up with what you did. Do you see?"

"But I think if we were just animals there," he answered quietly, " if we just think of ourselves, we would have killed each other in a fight, or each one go his own way. But we are human beings. I think that's the reason why it worked."

And then he really let me have it.

"But I appreciate very much that you are sincere and you told me your feeling. I always fight for the people to say what they feel. *Not only nice things.*" And with that, he stood up and walked out of the studio, but not before all that pique and pain and hostility had gone out over the air. To this moment I still feel some guilt for demanding introspection. Parrado and Canessa didn't owe me – or anybody – an accounting of their thoughts or motives. Of course, I remain fascinated by who survives and how they do so, and I always have been – long before cannibalism in the Andes and long before the Marten Hartwell story.

Hartwell, you remember, was the German bush pilot who crashed in the Arctic while on a mercy flight, bringing a British nurse, Judy Hill, a sick Eskimo boy, and his pregnant aunt to hospital. After a nineteen-day search, that plane was given up for lost, on the grounds that a human being couldn't possibly survive in that frozen wasteland for more than a very short time.

It could be argued that Hartwell would not have been a survivor at all had it not been for some of us at *As It Happens*. We stayed with the story of the lost plane after everybody else, including Air Rescue, had gone on to better things. I'm convinced that it was our broadcasting of the plea of Hartwell's girlfriend, Susan Haley, that persuaded James Richardson, then Minister of Defence, to launch that final, successful search.

Within hours of Hartwell's rescue, and the news that the three others on board had died, we began to get the upsetting story of cannibalism – and worse – from our northern stringer. Maybe because we felt a part of Hartwell's survival, maybe because we didn't want to believe it, we didn't broadcast what we were hearing. Cannibalism in South America, perhaps, but on Canadian soil – unthinkable. None of my arguments for staying with the story, nor the lobbying of an equally intrigued colleague, Richard Bronstein, convinced the others. Each morning Richard would come huffing into the story conference with the latest bulletin from the north. And each day his proposals were shot down. Hartwell might have resorted to cannibalism, but if we said so, *that* would be in bad taste.

Well, much of life is in bad taste and our rejection of the story did not change the facts of Hartwell's survival. It also didn't prevent the story from becoming a lurid, international scandal. The details were played for all they were worth, in good taste and in bad. Top mark in the latter category has to go to the headline writer in London who came up with this classic for *News of the World*: "Ex-Luftwaffe Pilot Eats British Nurse."

The question of taste is always a problem in doing survivor stories. When terrible things happen to people, and you decide to report on them, all the not-nice questions are there, absolutely explicit, whether you've got the gumption to ask them or not. It's an awful game between you and your guest. In your head you can almost hear them muttering to themselves, "I wonder how this one's going to put it? How's this one going to ask me how I managed to eat my friends?" Sometimes I'm amazed that survivors tell you anything at all. Most people won't share intimate experiences with people who are closest to them, never mind with some lady on the telephone from Canada whom they've never seen and with whom they will never have to deal again.

With Jean Pasqualini there were some additional problems. He felt his English inadequate to describe what he had suffered. He also knew his tale of starvation and forced labour in a Chinese prison camp wasn't timely; relations with Peking were becoming friendlier and people in the West were going China-crazy. Despite his name, Pasqualini is Chinese, the son of a Chinese mother and French father. He was charged with espionage in the fifties, when he decided to stay at his job with the United States army after the revolution. It was his father's citizenship and his own

French passport that ultimately saved him – although it took six years to do it. His lack of bitterness and the plainness of his narrative move me as often as I read what he said.

Mr. Pasqualini, there's just so much incredible detail in your story. Could we begin by talking about the use of the confession?

Fine. When you're arrested you're told you are guilty right off. You are told that the first morning by the team leader himself. He says, "You know where you are. This is a prison for counter-revolutionists. Whether you like it or not you are one." Then a few hours later, when you appear before the interrogator, he asks you, "Do you know where you are?" And, of course, you say, "Yes, I know where I am." He says, "Do you know why you have been arrested?" And, of course, most of the prisoners say, "No." And then he says, "Do you mean to tell me we've made a mistake in arresting you?"

And this is where we are faced with a dilemma. If we say we know, then we have to start talking. And if we say we don't, then we are accusing the government of making a mistake. So rather than accuse the government and thus aggravate our case, we say, all right, we have committed the crimes. And then we start telling them what crimes. Of course, the confessions in a Chinese prison do not take hours. The process takes weeks, months, and sometimes years.

It's almost like a perverse form of psychoanalysis. Mr. Pasqualini, I was amazed to read that physical coercion is strictly forbidden. And yet you write of constant hunger, which is physical coercion, isn't it?

Food is used as a weapon to break you down. The rations given to a prisoner in China are just enough to keep him alive. He's got a permanent feeling of hunger. He gets weak, not only physically but morally as well. He gets very selfish. And the authorities have one thing which we Westerners do not have, and that is an incredible amount of patience and a lot of time. This is what you call their trump card.

What happens when you're summoned after such a long period of waiting?

When you see your interrogator after such a long absence you're ready to kiss him, to say anything. The interrogator reminds you that the rations are the most you can expect from the government, and then he adds this: "We can wait a couple of months, a couple of years, if necessary, or even ten years, but we are sure that you can't." And this is where we all break down. Because hunger is a terrible feeling. Sometimes we prisoners even write notes asking to be interrogated. When you hear this now, it is a bit tragic. In those days it was not tragic at all. It was something which was really necessary. It's the only means for us to get out of the place.

What happened to your body, Mr. Pasqualini?

Well, you lose weight very, very quickly. We had to sit all the time. We became so emaciated. We had no more fat on our buttocks and every time we'd see a person being sent to the labour camps where we heard people were eating more, we felt envy, and at the same time, despair.

What is involved in making a confession?

The Chinese never have an official take down your statement. You accuse yourself. The name of the accuser and the name of the man being accused are you yourself. And this paper, which is going to hit the nail into your coffin, we actually received with a little joy in our hearts. Every time a guy in our cell was told to write his own accusation, it was like a feast. If we had had the means to do so, we'd have celebrated with champagne. Little did we realize that by writing such a document we were sending ourselves to prison for a long, long time.

So the confession, then, is not a simple thing like an admission of a crime. You're actually writing your own prescription for a process of reform.

Yes. In China a man must be proven guilty by his own words, because if anything in the statement suggests that the government played a part in a confession, it would no longer be valid in their own eyes. Once the interrogation is over, the prisoner is forced to read all the denunciation written against him, to prove to him that the state had a case against him all along, so that later on in the labour camps he will not bear any grudge against the government.

I think that anyone, Mr. Pasqualini, who throws the word "brainwashing" around loosely simply must read your story, because it's a much more sophisticated process than I think anyone has ever realized before. And yet you came out respecting what the Chinese were doing.

What seems very strange to the people in the West is that the prisoners and the guards co-exist peacefully. We prisoners knew and the guards knew that they could not drive us too hard. For example, one day a young warder, just out of the police academy, was put to work looking over us, watching us, and he started pestering us, telling us, "Hurry up, or else I'm going to put you in irons. Hurry up, or we're going to send you to the punishment brigade. You people are a bunch of slackers, I'm going to cut down your food rations by half."

Some of the veterans were sick and tired of him — by veterans I mean people who had been in prison more than ten years — and during the lunch break one of the veterans came over to the new warder and said, "Listen, Brigade Chief, it's no use you prodding us like this, no use to threaten us. Because, tell me, how many solitary cells have you got? Not more than a dozen. How many pairs of handcuffs have you got? Not more than fifty. Well, we are 185. And even if you were to send us all to the punitive brigade, who's going to be left to do the work? And if we don't finish our work, the plan is going to be affected. And if the plan's going to be affected, Mr. Warder, you're going to be with us next year, working alongside of us. So be smart."

It's incredible. That means that the prisoner is not a degraded animal, and in fact had been re-processed into thinking the right way.

There's another thing which is quite amazing. The Chinese communists, if they know they are beaten, they will accept defeat. For example, to show how human they were: I remember during 1961, during those bad years, we prisoners used to talk among ourselves about having a bit more to eat, about having a few more privileges, until one day the warder called me up to the office and said, "Look, if you people got any problems, if you people got any requests, if you got any difficulties, it's no use talking among yourselves, because you'll never find any solution. Come to us, come to the government, because if we can solve your problems we will, and if we can grant your requests we will. If we can't we will at least give you an explanation." That's the thing that really impressed us.

That sounds like many prisoners accept their prisoner status as almost a permanent condition. Are people finally released? Do they go home to their families?

Oh, no, they don't go home. They are so conditioned that on the day they graduate — we don't say that they are released we say they are "graduated" — they ask to be allowed to remain in the labour unit and to continue working there, living there as a free worker.

Thousands were dying around you. The system set out to destroy any friendships that might grow up among you. It rewarded mutual surveillance, and yet when you were sick and almost died, one man called Longfellow risked his life to save yours. Why do you think he did it?

Well, it was not one man, it was the entire cell of nineteen people. This fellow came to see me when I was almost dying on that pallet of straw in the sick bay, with the stink coming in from the outside and the flies all around. He slipped three eggs into my hand. The others caught frogs and looked for wild vegetables. They even stole rice from the fields and made a stew for me. This continued for months.

Why, do you think?

When I returned to the unit, I went to the cell leader, Longfellow. I say, "Longfellow, I like to thank you for all that you and the rest of the cell mates have done for me." He looked at me and he said, "You don't have to thank me. Tell me one thing. How many were we when this brigade was formed?" I say, "We were 270." He says, "Good. How many are left today?" I say, "Seventeen." And he says, "Seventeen. If we can do something to make one victim less, we'll do it." And, with a sweep of his hand, this man said to me, "Look at all these people. All these people including myself will never be able to get out of here, but you're special. You have a slight chance of getting out, not only out of here but also out of China. And that is why we have seen to it. We hope that once you're out, you'll tell the world what's happening here. That is why we've kept you alive."

When you were finally released and deported from China, did you undergo yet another transformation so that you could survive as a free man again?

No. I found I was able to readjust myself quite quickly. But I must say I am a different man from what I was before my arrest. I live very much in the past, because every time I get myself discontented, dissatisfied, I say to myself, "Where were you ten years ago?" And I immediately realize how wrong I am to complain, you see.

Once, someone asked me what happiness is for me. And I said, "Happiness for me is to be able to eat as much as I want, when I want, whatever I want." But I must say that I came out of the prison camp a much better man than when I went in. It may sound a bit strange, but I got more out of them than they got out of me.

Survivors will tell their stories if they can do it on their own terms — which means sharing the details of their suffering, but rarely talking about how they stood it. For every Tiede Herrema (the Dutch businessman held by IRA gunmen for endless weeks in 1975), who would have nothing to do with the press when he was released and who immediately retreated into anonymity, there are many more who need — or want — to confirm their survival publicly. Some have a political point to make and talking to the press turns out to be a very effective way of taking political vengeance. Some find interviews a way of piecing off their suffering, giving the rest of us some pain. For a few, I'm sure, talking is a way of dealing with the guilt of surviving when others couldn't.

Obviously, there's enormous difficulty in interviewing people who've suffered a great deal. When someone's been on the other side, he's forever marked by what happened there. These people know — and you know — that no matter how much we say that we sympathize, we can never really understand. No wonder they try to protect the uniqueness of their experience. No wonder they resent those who presume to have shared the horror by merely hearing about it.

I once spoke to the articulate and politicized Iranian writer and poet, Dr. Reza Baraheni, for example. He was arrested in Iran in 1973 and held for three and a half months by SAVAK, the Iranian secret police, for his political position. He had been mercilessly frank in this interview in detailing the physical torments of the Shah's prisons. But notice how reserved he becomes when I want him to share the emotional torment he experienced during his detention.

How did you cope with the fear, Dr. Baraheni?

It's a gradual thing, you know. You do it almost step by step. You suffer. You hope at the same time. I tried to be very realistic and very tactful, not heroic at all, because I didn't feel like a hero. I thought that it was suffering of the worst kind, but it wasn't only me. There are 100,000 political prisoners now in Iran.

What finally breaks you? Is it the pain, the brutality, or the humiliation?

I think it's the humiliation.

Can you talk about that?

Well, you really feel that you are nothing, even if you may have been someone outside, even if you may have been respected — even if you may have written twenty or thirty books of prose and poetry. You see that a totally illiterate man can simply put his foot on you and smash you in the way he would smash an ant. You are always blindfolded, you can't see, and you have to depend on the guard, whom you don't know and who can take you anywhere.

Why doesn't a person just give up? What in you survives and fights back?

I think that depends. I know of people who put their heads under their blankets and simply chew their own blood veins in their wrists and die at night in prison. Or a person whose fingernails had been taken out one by one; when they come after him in order to take him for the tenth fingernail, he actually puts it in their hands and says, "You see, I've done this last night myself." There are people who are very courageous and there are people who aren't very courageous.

Whenever we talk on this program to someone who has gone through the most terrible events, as you have, they never sound as though they hate their torturers. Can you explain how that could be?

Well, having been a writer and also having been in the world of politics, I think that it's not a personal resentment that really matters in this day.

But it's unreal to not hate, it's unreal.

I hate them, I hate all of them. If you see the prison poems which I have written, I actually deal with each of them. It's a poetry of hatred and poetry of, I would say, spite.

It just astounds me always that people can come through an experience like that and function at all.

I think perhaps a person who has been tortured and has had that experience, when he comes out, he's happy that he's alive. At the same time he has hopes, because he's experienced what it is to come out and he has stood alone.

And that means what?

That means life. I'm a very optimistic type of person. I'm looking ahead to a better future for the people of the country and I want to expose what is happening there, because no other writer is going to do that.

Louise Stratton is a survivor of another sort. Stratton was one of fifteen people held hostage in June, 1975, in a tiny vault at the British Columbia Penitentiary. Her captors were three desperate lifers, Andy Bruce, Dwight Lucas, and Claire Wilson. The incident ended when an armed squad burst in, overwhelmed the convicts, and fatally shot Stratton's coworker and fellow hostage, Mary Steinhauser. I talked to Stratton within hours of that bloody finale, when she was still reeling from the horror of Steinhauser's death, and was already the subject of headlines and questions in the House of Commons implying improper intimacy with Claire Wilson.

Stratton stared down the entire country in that conversation. In a forthright, almost defiant way, she told us more about being a hostage than we had ever known before. Unlike most survivors, she was willing to break the survivors' code and expose what was going on in her mind during that nightmarish siege.

The interview was never broadcast. Once again, good taste reared its pretty face and defeated all arguments for airing what its critics now concede is a valuable document. I think there was some fear that we would be condemned by our audience for exploiting Stratton's vulnerability, and some worry that Stratton's openness, and her refusal to disguise the less flattering details, might sound like a tacky postscript on a tragic story. I still believe that that decision was misguided, and so I print the interview here for what I've always believed it to be – a legacy from an honest human being, caught without warning by calamity.

Miss Stratton, I don't want to fence around with you. I think everybody in the country tonight wants to know not about what went on in that vault so much as how it is possible. How is it possible for a woman, given the kind of pressure that must have been on you, to develop a positive – maybe a sexual – relationship with one of her captors?

It is possible because I was thinking of number one – myself. I saw him. I saw his eyes. He saw me. He saw my eyes. And I said, "Stratton, if there's an out for you, it's through him." And that's how it started. He was a human being. He was close to me. He assured me that I wouldn't get hurt and so it became very real and very possible. The whole situation was so completely and totally unreal that nothing seemed irregular.

Did you maybe come on to him a bit, too?

Most definitely. I mean, for sure I did.

So a lot of what happened was your idea?

I would say it was quite mutual.

I still don't understand.

Well, I can't even explain it. His eyes were not the eyes of a man who was about to blitz fifteen people. His eyes were – they looked at me with tenderness, with a feeling of, "What in hell are you and I doing in a place like this?"

So it was romantic.

Most definitely romantic. Yes. And I think I used him, to a certain extent.

In what sense?

Well, I used him because I wanted to be close to him for my own self-protection. Also, if he were under my control, that's one less person who's threatening us. And then it became very obvious that he would not present a problem of that sort, ever.

And then, from that sense of relief, a sexual relationship took off between you, with the other hostages watching this?

Yeah, I suppose, if you mean tenderness, being close — his gently holding a knife at my throat, or my wiping the sweat from his forehead. If that's what you mean by a sexual encounter, yeah. Some of that they saw. If you mean my kissing him, yeah. If you mean my holding him, yeah. Is that what you meant?

Yup, that's what I meant. You see, it's very hard for any of us to understand what we would do. Most people cannot believe that they could possibly be sexually aroused in a situation like that.

Well, I'm not really sure either, but the demerol I was given could have had a lot to do with it. It really could have.

But it began with coercion and the threat of force. So how can you like somebody that does that to you? How is that possible?

Well, because first of all, I could identify with the position that he was in. It was as though he was saying, "For me it's all over." He saw that he had nothing left for him, period, and so he had nothing to lose. He couldn't identify with anybody he was taking hostage. He was probably — I think, I don't know for sure — on drugs when he started. And I was on drugs most of the time. I didn't take so much that I didn't know what was going on, but enough to make everything seem relatively okay.

You make it sound like you were just a social worker caring for him — identifying, supporting, being sympathetic. Was that the extent of it? Or was it different?

> I don't understand what you mean. You mean, was I in love with him? Was I emotionally involved with him?

I guess so.

> There was definitely emotional involvement. But it was a situational thing. I suppose I loved him in a sense. That doesn't mean that I love him now — or would love him now — or that I would have loved him before. It was just a completely situational thing that has no bearing on the past or the future. I cannot even explain it. And it was initiated by my desire to save my own skin.

Is there no punishment of yourself when you emerge from an experience like this?

> I suppose there is a little punishment, but not — no, I don't think there is, only in the sense that I know that, because of it, I didn't go through as much hell as everybody else did. So there's that kind of punishment. But had I not gone through what I went through, there would have been a lot more hell for everybody. And I felt that they understood that. Really, I did.

There was a statement attributed to you when the authorities came in with guns. Something like, "Was that a bull?"

> Right, I said that. I was very confused and I guess I was trying to decipher whether or not things were going in our favour or against us.

Who's us? I guess that's where I was heading with that. Had you always called guards "bulls"?

> No, definitely not.

So what happened, locked up there, do you think, to change your head?

> I don't think anything changed my head.

You haven't changed your orientation? You haven't begun to identify as someone on the inside?

> No, not any more than I ever did. I mean, I would not be functional in my job if I didn't identify with the inmates to a certain extent. People are making such a big deal out of something that is human, natural. It was a show of feeling, of emotion, compassion. I don't understand why they're so concerned, I really don't.

I think people are just puzzled. We don't know what we'd do. So we're all smart guys.

> I suppose. I thought I was, too. I never imagined that the kind of person that I would be dealing with would be a person like Claire Wilson. I envisioned people as more the heavy Dwight Lucas type.

Why did you leave the penitentiary in the early hours of Wednesday morning screaming and crying, and why did you refuse to go to the debriefing?

> I think, primarily, that was just the breaking point. I don't mean a nervous breakdown, as I've heard rumoured. But it just all had to come out and it came out in anger, perhaps partially as a result of the confusion. It's partly empathy for two of the three inmates. There's certainly deep feeling for Mary and the fact that she had to be the one that was ultimately sacrificed. I don't even know if that's a good word to use. If there's anger, it's definitely towards Lucas and maybe a little bit over the fact that we were so cut off. We really had the feeling that nobody cared and that they weren't doing all that they could.

Miss Stratton, is any of it an anger that your life really has changed now? Are you kind of straddling here? You're no longer in there. The world didn't end in those forty-one hours. And now you've got to live on the outside with this locked inside of you.

> No, because I've been through other things that have been traumatic. I feel very confident and self-assured.

Did you ever enter Wilson's fantasy about getting out of there together? Taking a helicopter to another country? Did you believe it? Want it?

> I believed that it would happen. But not as they hoped. And I explained that to him. This was here and now and what we felt was a result of the situation that we were in. When we weren't in that situation anymore, obviously the whole thing was going to be a new ballgame. He understood that, and he never argued or threatened or hurt me or forced me to do anything.

You know, it's kind of awkward talking like this. It's really awful, because I don't want you to think I'm judging you, because none of us wants to be in the jam that you were in.

I'm not in a jam. Why am I in a jam?

I mean in that room.

Oh, I thought you meant now. No – I don't mind that the whole world judges me, either.

Not everybody's sex life makes it to *Hansard*. And that must be awful.

Perhaps. And it will be. But at the moment it isn't.

Miss Stratton, I hope that things work out for you.

Thank you. I think they will.

That your life comes out okay and that this works for you.

I appreciate that. And I appreciate your concern.

Six
Who's Out There?

For a while there, our show became the one dependable spot on the radio dial for people who like to follow the arrivals, departures, and flying patterns of the silver ships from outer space. Exactly why our crew of committed journalists has experienced some of its happiest moments chasing down UFO stories I leave to others to decide. I can only report that somehow a rivalry developed within the unit over who could turn up the most far-out outer-space theory. As a result, I must by now have talked to everyone who's ever seen a flying saucer, been on a flying saucer, or theorized about one.

Maybe because I'm not a UFO believer myself, I've never been able to grasp the pattern or the purpose of these inter-species meetings. The aliens certainly seem to be selective about whom to make their presence known to. It's never a group of scientists at a university, for example, but always some hapless couple driving down a lonesome country road.

When I worried over that one with Stanton Friedman, a California physicist who bills himself the Ralph Nader of the UFO, he didn't seem surprised at all.

"Why in the world would any rational person want to particularly contact a group of scientists at a university campus?" was the way he put it.

"Well," I countered, "to exchange information, perhaps."

"What are we going to give them?" he laughed.

He had me there.

Friends of the flying saucer, like the good galactic neighbours that they are, live in perpetual readiness, watching and waiting for the first silvery humanoids to finally land and stay. While they wait, their other-worldly studies keep them busy and broadminded, engagingly free of the egocentric notion, which torments the rest of us Earthlings, that we alone people God's universe. If their flying-saucer research leads to nothing more definitive than proof of the need for more investigation, why, that's fine. Really, it's the questions that they enjoy. Conclusions tend to be confining, anyway. Besides, they have the comfort of knowing that at least somebody's in charge, somebody's out there who knows what he's doing and even has time, it seems, to keep one eye on us.

For their sakes, I hope that no one ever solves the mysteries of inter-stellar flight and spoils the fun of UFO study. Like the people who pursue the Loch Ness Monster or track the yeti and the sasquatch, UFO fans deserve nothing but more tantalizing trails.

One of the most original UFO tales I've heard is the stunning thesis that the Third Reich is alive and well and living on flying saucers under the ice of Antarctica. It comes from the brain-storming of a German immigrant to Canada, Christoff Friedrich, a balding, dishevelled, bookkeeperish looking man. He arrived at our studio sweaty with excitement and grateful for the chance to lay finally before a national audience a wealth of documentation accumulated over twenty years.

Out of two tattered valises poured a lifetime's collection of yellowed clippings, faded World-War-Two aerial photographs, and reprints from old Nazi engineering textbooks, which together suggested to Friedrich a possibility so out-in-front that he'd been obliged to publish it himself.

Mr. Friedrich, it's hard to believe that someone could link Hitler and the UFO, our two favourite subjects on *As It Happens*.

I think I have a winning combination. I have analysed the flying saucer story from all the various conventional angles. From space travel, to the idea that they come here to stop us from experimenting with atomic weapons, or that they come down here to plant another civilization. None of this stuff makes sense.

What's your theory?

Germany had flying saucers in World War Two. I know that for a fact because a German major who worked in Goering's department, where he evaluated flying saucers, convincingly showed me engineering drawings, prototype photographs, and data that he said were part of the German saucer story. These were the miracle weapons that Hitler spoke of. And this is what set me on the trail, because usually with Goebbels and Hitler, there was a smidgin of truth in what they were saying.

Your Nazi unidentified flying objects — where are they coming from?

The poles.

The poles.

The poles.

I mean, what would they live off on the poles?

These flying saucers have the capability to pick up food, nourishment, anything like this. But it's not only that they have bases in the poles; there's the Shaverian theory, which is a very well-known theory, that there is a civilization in inner Earth and the poles are the entrance to it.

You don't believe this.

Well, Shaver says so and —

But you don't believe that, do you?

I speculate on that Barbara. I speculate on that.

There wouldn't be a penguin left if they had to live at the poles.

Not really, I have a map that shows the immense expanse of the polar regions.

Let's say that they are there. What are they doing?

Monitoring. Waiting for the day, as Hitler said in one of his last prophetic speeches, that there surely is going to be a clash between East and West, because these two giant systems are incompatible. And then "we will be the tip on the scales." You see, right now they don't have the manpower to do anything physical.

I don't doubt that many Nazi officers are still alive and still grieving. But that doesn't put them under the ice on a UFO.

It does in a way, Barbara, because it does mean that there is a segment of the population at any given time that is prone to this kind of thinking.

Prove it. Prove they're at the South Pole. You've got this whole photo album; what have you got in there?

Right. For instance, we have this story here. The man took a lie detector test. His name is Reinhold Schmidt. He's an American of German background. He was taken up in a flying saucer to the poles to their base. And he says that the crew spoke German. They were dressed like you and I. They looked like you and I. But he says that when these people spoke among themselves they used high German, which I happen to understand.

But that could be one guy's nightmare, okay?

If you want hard evidence, I have never been down to Antarctica myself, I've never been taken on a German saucer down there. But the hard fact is that the Germans did have flying saucers. They tested them. They could fly them. We have the data on how they looked — the speeds they achieved, and so on.

What's their plan?

World War Two is not ended. There is at this time no peace treaty between the warring nations of World War Two and Germany today. That's why you read about all the United States Air Force planes chasing saucers, and shoot-to-kill orders, and stuff like that. That would only make sense. There's no other logical explanation for it, Barbara. None whatsoever.

If Hitler was so smart and if the Third Reich had this other-wordly, thirty-years-ahead type of equipment, why did they lose the war?

Too little too late.

A-hah.

You see, first they concentrated on rocketry. The theory is that the Allies would leap on the German rocketry development and expend all of their technological effort into this one firecracker direction. Whereas the Germans would be off in the wild blue yonder developing the UFO.

So Wernher von Braun was a Nazi plot against America? He didn't know.

I don't think he does to this day.

You're right. He still doesn't know. I wrote to him about it. He says, "Oh, no, I know nothing about that."

When the Nazis go out for little jaunts to test the motors, why do they buzz people on the highways?

No, no. These are constant surveillance flights, undoubtedly. That's why you always see them close to Pickering, and other atomic research stations. You see a fantastic amount over Northern Russia, where you have these big camps.

The Nazis are checking out the competition?

Keeping in touch. Keeping in touch.

Over the years the US military has been accused of many deceptions, but few as brazen as the cover-up charged by UFO specialist Dr. Robert Carr. Since 1948, says Carr, the American Air Force has deliberately kept from the world evidence that would have proven that UFO experts have been right all along. He says that flying saucers are real and that governments have used ridicule and The Big Lie as tools of a massive and blatant cover-up.

I did not learn of Carr's charges through any of our regular channels. The story came from my housekeeper. She arrived one morning insisting that four little green men had just been captured and were being held at a military base somewhere in the US — she thought Ohio, maybe. When I arrived with that intelligence, the *As It Happens* machine went into action. Within the hour we had zeroed in on the source of my housekeeper's news and had him on the line.

Carr was noticeably exasperated, fed up with waiting for the military to tell the world the truth about flying saucers. If nobody else had the courage to take on the powers that be,

Carr himself would do it. While I de-briefed him, our producers set to work to find someone at the air force base to respond to these extraordinary charges.

Dr. Carr, where is the military hiding this secret?
> In Ohio, at Wright-Patterson Air Force Base, Dayton, Ohio, in building number eighteen – in the maximum security section where atomic weapons are kept. They have two captured flying saucers. One is in almost perfect condition, except for one porthole, which has been smashed. The occupants died of decompression. The other flying saucer wasn't found right away and it's half destroyed and burned. That one had four badly charred bodies in it. I've never been able to find out what they did with them. I hope they buried them, but the complete bodies from the unburnt ship were put into deep freeze, just as human beings are put in cryonic preservation.

What kind of authority are you hearing this from?
> Well, I'm hearing it from eyewitness reports. I got a call from an executive with an important organ of the media, who often visited Wright-Patterson and co-operated with them on many stories. Yet when he asked to be admitted to building eighteen in the maximum security section, they just froze up.

Those bodies that you say are deep-frozen – how long have they been in the deep freeze?
> They've been there since 1948, when they were found about three miles from Aztec, New Mexico.

So this new news is very old news indeed?
> But the new news is this: the flying saucer cover-up down here in the United States has become so cumbersome, so unworkable, that both the CIA and the Air Intelligence want to dump the thing next month. They want to get out from under it and admit that the flying saucers have always been real. Flying saucers are crossing our skies, they're landing. Reputable witnesses are having confrontations with flying-saucer occupants. And yet a general sits in the Pentagon monotonously repeating to phone callers that there are no such things as flying saucers.

I should tell you that we're trying to get through right now to that base, as we talk to you. I don't know if we'll get a word from them tonight.

> Fine, but you're wasting your time. I can tell you now what you'll get. You'll get the monotonous and utterly ludicrous denial of something that most informed people know is true.

While we're waiting, Professor Carr, those bodies in the deep freeze – any eyewitness reports on what they look like?

> Yes, there are a number of eyewitness reports, because they've been seen by a number of scientists. They're perfectly formed males between three and four feet –

Hold it, Professor Carr, we've got a Captain Bowman on the line right now, from the Wright-Patterson Air Force Base. Hang on. Captain Bowman? Hello? I'm waiting. Hello? I think he hung up on us. Hello?

> Look, Madame, if you could find one US government official willing to confirm what I am telling you, you would still only be getting last week's news. What I am telling you is next month's news. You don't believe that any of these people in official positions are going to confirm what I'm saying. They will deny it.

Let's see if Captain Bowman is there. Hello? Hello? I guess he just left the line when he heard you talking about those three- to four-foot-high men in the deep freeze.

> Well, of course, he left the line. He has to live with this thing every day. It must be very uncomfortable. They have to rotate their public relations officers very rapidly down there because the strain is so great.

I don't understand, Professor Carr, how you can keep three- to four-foot tiny bodies in a cryogenic solution since 1948 and have nobody know about it.

> I didn't say nobody knew about it. I said the secret is so well known it has become laughable. They are formed like human beings and they are in superb physical condition. The only anomaly that was pointed out was found by a brain surgeon, who upon opening the skull of the one that was dissected said that, according to the convolutions of the brain – the number of wrinkles and the depth of the wrinkles – the subject must be several

hundred years old. Yet he appeared to be a young man in the pink of physical condition. Perhaps on their planet our rules don't apply.

What's important now is that the president must immediately cancel the shoot-to-kill orders that the air force is now operating under. We hope that with Barry Goldwater as a spearhead, the president will be moved to set aside a safe landing zone in the southwestern desert, clearly marked, where by signs and symbols it's perfectly clear there is no treachery, no hidden guns, no ambush, no murder, and for once the human race can come forward and meet these visitors from another world with a dignity befitting *Homo sapiens*.

Professor Carr, let us absorb all of this and get back to you.

What keeps the UFO story moving along is the succession of perfectly believable, straight-ahead types who report the most totally unbelievable, un-straight-ahead events. One of the most credible I've ever talked to was Mike Rogers, an Arizona lumberjack, who watched helplessly with his fellow-workers in 1975 while a hovering saucer zapped his buddy, Travis Walton, with a terrifying blue ray. I talked to Rogers right after he took a lie-detector test; the Snowflake, Arizona, sheriff had suspected that there must be a more conventional cause for poor Walton's disappearance. I talked to Rogers a day or two after the incident.

Mr. Rogers, has anyone heard from Walton yet?
　I've heard rumours that they have, yes.
Alive and well?
　Yes, and they say that he was definitely taken into a UFO. I can't really tell you anything more about it. I don't want to state that it is fact yet.
All right. Why don't you tell us what you saw?
　We saw a lighted object just to the side of the road up in front of us. As we approached the thing we realized it was a UFO of some kind. It was hovering about fifteen feet above the ground. We estimate that it was about fifteen feet in diameter and about eight feet high from top to

bottom. Although it appeared to be a disc, from the side
it had an oval appearance. When I looked out the window I was quite surprised to find that it was so near,
almost on top of us. Then I saw Walton running over
toward the object.

What happened with this blue ray?

As Walton approached the object and got up under the
rim, it started making a noise that sounded like it had
started its engines or something. It sounded like a
water-driven generator or some kind of pump. At the
same time, it started a yawing and pitching motion.
Walton made a couple more steps toward the object
when a laser beam or some kind of ray, which we've all
concluded looked about two feet wide, came out of the
bottom of the UFO and struck Walton. It was like an
explosion going off in front of him. It blew him back and
he hit the ground about ten feet back.

What's Walton like?

He's about six feet and one inch tall and he's slender,
although quite heavy-chested due to body building and
muscle training. He believes in health foods and he's a
fanatic about health. He won't touch cigarettes or al-
cohol or any kind of drugs. He only eats certain foods
that are what he considers to be healthy.

Was he a kook?

No, he was a very level-headed person, very intelligent.
He had a genius IQ.

Did the other guys like him?

Yes, I don't know of anybody who didn't. Some of the
dummies in the group kind of resented his intellectual
conversations during break-time and the like. I don't
mean that anybody hated him or anything like that. Of
course, the people in this town and in this country have
all thought – until we passed our lie-detector tests yes-
terday – that we had probably done him in and hidden
him and made up this story. But I think they are all
feeling different, now.

What are Walton's relatives thinking?

Well, his brother had something like this happen to him
a few years back. He was chased through the woods by
one approximately twelve years ago.

They're really after this family.

Oh, many people in this area have had numerous sightings, even I've had sightings. I think it's because of the area in which we live and work.

Mr. Rogers, I hope we find poor Walton.

The fantastic possibility that the men of outer space keep coming here because they lust after human women has been revealed by American UFO investigator Lehmann Hisey. Mr. Hisey is the author of the metaphysical classic, *Keys to Inner Space.*

Mr. Hisey, why would UFO people be raping our women? That's an angle we've never heard before.

Because their energy has run out and they no longer can reproduce human forms. So if they can plant a seed here, they will have something to tune in on.

Are they going to come back for their offspring?

In fact, they're walking around now.

Their offspring are among us?

Oh, yes.

What do they look like?

I thought I saw one at a space convention recently. They look like anybody else, but they have a very strange sort of an aura and they just look different. It's the feeling that you have about them. You have a feeling that they're not of this planet, perhaps because something has been implanted in their bodies that can transmit information to the mother ship.

We've got some pretty spaced-out people working on this program of ours. You should come and investigate some of them.

Yes. Well, that will all come in due time.

How do you get this kind of inside information?

I have a tape that I'm not at liberty to release, which came through a little man outside of Phoenix, a farm person. His wife looked at him one night and he looked very strange. He said, "I am Ishcamar." She called a friend of mine in Phoenix and he went out and taped this man. He turned out to be the commander of a spaceship some hundred thousand miles out.

You mean a spaceship commander had taken possession of a poor farmer in Phoenix?

Yes, I made two or three tapes and they're absolutely terrific.

Has this commander given you any of their military secrets?

No military secrets. But he said that very soon they will make themselves known in a very practical way.

Are they coming to save us or to hurt us?

Well, they can't save us. They could not evacuate us because we cannot exist in outer space. We're not physically equipped for it. Chemically, we couldn't get off the ground. So we're stuck here, whatever happens.

Keep your eyes open, Mr. Hisey.

The image of a captured UFO personage condemned to ride around Wisconsin as a Cadillac hood ornament is one of the nice legacies of *As It Happens*. If only it had ended there. Unfortunately, Edward Ben Elson, who told us the story, turned out to be a fake, not into the UFO scene at all but on a bandwagon for better treatment of the mentally ill. As soon as he tried to move from his UFO experience to his spiel on tolerance, I was so let down that I did a crazy thing myself — I cut the interview short. It was five days before Christmas and everybody had had their fill of messages.

How are you, Mr. Elson?

As well as can be expected.

Sure.

On Monday this flying saucer landed on our property and a glorious ten-foot person, who could have been male or female, entered our house carrying bushel baskets. He made ten trips in all. We were too awestruck and terror-stricken to try to communicate with this personage. Only later, we went downstairs and discovered in our basement miniaturized human beings. They were in some type of suspended-animation state, because when I tried to pick one of them up to examine it more closely, I discovered its incredible weight. With the help of my wife I put this little male figurine on our bathroom scale and he weighed 165 pounds. A female figurine weighed 114 pounds.

Do you mean you have ten bushel baskets full of little people down in your basement as we're speaking?

No, I don't. The wire services were incorrect about that. I said they were delivered. But truthfully they're not here any more. What happened is that my wife, Patricia, sold one of them to a local Cadillac dealer. He bought it apparently as a hood ornament for his Cadillac car. Subsequently the UFO personage came back and took the ten bushel baskets away.

Why, do you figure?

For safe keeping. To keep them out of the hands of my wife. She's very materialistic, you know.

It was at this point that he launched into his pitch for mental health and I cut him off.

I was studying my research for an interview about remotely-controlled "ghost planes" with John Taylor, the editor of *All the World's Aircraft,* when all of a sudden it hit me. Mr. Taylor, describing these new weapons, could have been mistaken for one of our UFO "scientists." When I suggested to Taylor that his RPV missiles seemed able to do a lot of things that flying saucers are famous for, he got as excited about the implications as I was. And so, instead of talking about the RPV and *détente,* as we were scheduled to, we spent our time on what I still believe was the even hotter news angle – the true story of the UFO.

Mr. Taylor, when I first read about the RPV it sounded remarkably like a UFO. How many countries now have these and how many are developing them?

Something like six or seven countries at the moment. The main operator, of course, is America. There are some in the UK, some in Canada, some in Italy, Germany, and Japan. The Soviet Union has some. We know very little about theirs at the moment but they certainly have some. Why aren't they vulnerable to being tracked and chronicled?

Well, the little mini RPV that the Rand Company has produced, for example, doesn't have any straight lines anywhere. Every possible surface is curved, so if you pick it up by radar, you get what the radar people call "scatter." The signals don't bounce back towards your receiver. They go off into space. The RPV itself is made of plastic. If you were lucky enough to pick it up, it would look about the size of a very tiny bird.

But let me tell you a little story. I spoke to a very senior officer of an air force in Europe and said to him, "Do you have any evidence of Soviet RPV missiles flying over your country?" And he said, "You've seen reports in the press about UFO sightings over our country, haven't you?" So I said, "Yes." He said, "Well, do you believe in flying saucers?" "Not really." "Well, what else could they be, then?" And so I said, "Well, they could be RPV missiles. If you shot down a Soviet RPV, would you tell the press?" And his reply was, "When we shoot down things, we don't tell the press."

Not "if," but "when."

Right.

You're describing something with round sides, which can hover low. You haven't talked about sound. But you've written about laser beams and we're hearing about blue rays right now in Arizona. I just wonder if people are seeing the testing of the RPV when they sight a UFO.

I think this is quite likely, yes. Some of these aircraft are very, very quiet.

What about the low ones that hover, would they emit light?

You'd have light from the engines. You'd see the engine exhaust, so they would appear to emit light. You see, if you get any sort of light or any engine exhaust glowing through a damp atmosphere, you'll get a very peculiar sort of glow with a halo around it, very often.

People always say that UFOs can turn suddenly, that they can move suddenly, drift, loiter, hover, and then zoom away.

Well, not having a pilot on board, you can pull a very, very tight turn with an RPV. You can pull a much tighter turn and impose greater loads on it than you can on a piloted aircraft, because a man wouldn't survive. Therefore, they can turn remarkably quickly, yes.

Isn't that fascinating. You may be really onto something, Mr. Taylor.

Well, it could be, it's possible. Obviously, there are many things going on all the time in aviation that don't get highly publicized. The American reconnaissance aircraft, the SR-71, which is the fastest airplane ever to serve with any air force, was virtually unknown for years. The Secretary of State announced that it existed, but we didn't know it had already been tested and was in service by then. You can keep an aircraft like that very quiet if you want to.

Could that explain why authorities always pooh-pooh these sightings? Maybe this could account, too, for why some of these sightings are seen zooming along power lines and roads.

They could be test vehicles doing all sorts of jobs. Obviously, if you're going to test one of these aircraft, if you can get it to fly very accurately along one of your own power lines, you know how accurately you can control it over a long distance.

So running it along power lines makes sense as a test?

Oh, yes, along straight roads, just to test it, to test how stable it is, how well it will keep to a pre-programmed course, if it's going to be out of your control range. Already we have something like twenty or twenty-five variants of one design from the Rand Company. They were used extensively in Vietnam for reconnaissance and they brought back some very remarkable photographs.

Mr. Taylor, I have a feeling that you may have accounted for something that's been mysterious for a long, long time.

If you are troubled that millions of your fellow citizens believe in UFOs and would like someone to blame – blame the scientists. Blame all those astro-physicists and astronomers and micro-biologists who confound us with their theories. They're the ones who've trained us to believe. You laugh at poor Friedrich and his UFO Nazis under the polar cap? I've talked to a man, who is on the payroll of one of England's best universities, who insists there is something out there in space called a black hole; not one – many. One day very soon, he assures me, men and women are going to fly out in a space ship to one of those holes, hurl some metal over the rim, and then – with some giant tweezer in the sky – fish that now-energized metal out again and send its energy back down to Earth by microwave to keep our lamps and dishwashers going a little longer.

For a nineteenth-century mind like mine, that prospect's unreal. I march in the army of the credulous and cope with an idea like that in one of two ways: occasionally I take it, usually I leave it. It's believe or disbelieve. Comprehension's not an option. Given my problem – and a scientist to interview – I confess that I scurry as quickly as good manners allow through the data-seeking questions. I prefer to deal with scientists as personalities, concentrating on the questions that begin with "why" instead of "what" and "how."

Astronomers are especially responsive to that kind of interview. People who spend their nights searching for what's out there, men who are ready to mine outer space, or who are confident enough about the future to try to signal other intelligent life in the universe with messages that won't arrive in their lifetimes – never mind get answered – are exhilarating to talk to. We may feel annihilated contemplating the eons, extinguished by the infinity of space. The astronomer feels invigorated.

The expectation that knowledge can only bring good is part of the mind set of the top-quality scientist. And although I wouldn't want to push the comparison too far, all those UFO believers share at least that conviction with their more conventional counterparts in sky-watching. It's an optimism that was best expressed to me in a conversation with a physicist at Stanford who was trying to sort out the basic building blocks of matter. Like the astronomers who pursue things too big for us to comprehend, Burton Richter was losing me on the small. I asked him finally if his single-mindedness was maybe futile, anyway. Perhaps God was toying with him, condemning him to live in permanent frustration as he tried to solve His riddles. But Richter, like everyone else in the who-and-what's-out-there game, wasn't worried.

"No," he said simply, "physicists as a whole do not believe that God is mean. God is subtle, but God is not mean."

Lovely.

Seven
The Phoney War between the Sexes

The "phoney war" was the period between the autumn of 1939 and the spring of 1940, when Britain, France, and Germany were technically at war, but very little blood was being shed. In the war between the sexes we're into a comparable interval of artificial calm. The heavy guns on both sides have stopped their firing. Tempers are noticeably cooler. For the moment, anyway, what I find I'm covering on the radio is mostly fitful skirmishing. I suspect that when the economy is better and there is less political uncertainty, the struggle for women's rights will heat up again. But for now, at least, women seem content to consolidate early victories and savour their little bits of new-found power.

I must confess that in me, too, there's very little feminist fire still burning. For the life of me, I can't bring back the fury I used to feel in the Women's Lib debates that I initiated with friends – my husband included. The anger is just no longer there. Of course, I'm irritated by the fact that advertisers still sell to women by making us feel ugly and inadequate. I'm upset when the CBC, like every other employer, takes advantage of ambitious females who'll work twice as hard for equal pay. Sure, I get excited when my thirteen-year-old daughter wants to pierce her lovely ears.

And I'm unhappy that the notion of "women's work" still prevails – even among so-called "liberated" women.

The division of household labour was an issue much fought over but never resolved in the recent round of serious fighting. A lot of people, I think, are still hoping that they can leave it all to Wonderwoman – the woman who will juggle home and job and family and still have time and strength for fun and glamour. Well, it seems that Wonder-woman is tired and not coping all that well. Lately it's the independent types who seem to be making it – the women who will boldly tell you that they've paid their dues and now are free to chuck husband, home, and kids so that they can get on with the real job of living. Joann Vanek, an American researcher, studied the workload of married women and offers a good reason why Wonderwoman feels overwhelmed.

I think I like you, Miss Vanek.
   No kidding. Why?
Because I haven't noticed the workload going down, either.
   Are you married, Barbara?
Am I ever.
   How many kids?
Three. And two dogs.
   And a full-time job and a full house, not an apartment?
Correct.
   That's a lot of work.
And a nervous breakdown. That takes a day a week.
   What's the nervous breakdown from, the job?
From the extras. Why aren't all our labour-saving devices saving women any time?
   Because things break down and that takes extra work, waiting for people to fix them. That's one thing. Buying the things takes more time, too. These labour-saving devices create their own work. That's part of it –
Of course, today our husbands help us.
   No. Husbands do not help women. Husbands do roughly six, maybe seven hours of housework a week at the most, and most of that is shopping. And that's not necessarily shopping for groceries. It could be shopping for a family

television set or for their own clothes. Husbands like to do their own distinctive things. If a husband is going to help at all, it's doing stuff like fixing equipment, perhaps shovelling the sidewalks if there's snow, washing and drying dishes, and taking out garbage. But where housework has technology to help — dishwashers for example, or the garbage disposal — rather than freeing the wife, it frees the husband. Now he doesn't have to do that.

There's one part of your study I don't like. You ask why women with jobs can get their housework done in twenty-six hours a week, while women with no job use fifty-five hours to do the same thing.

Right.

But are they really doing the same thing? Don't women with jobs cut corners unbelievably?

I think so. I think oftentimes working women want to be Wonderwomen. So they just play up those parts of the job that they do well, not the real conflicts and difficulties.

What about child care? How much time does a woman today spend on child care compared to her mother or grandmother?

She spends more time than her mother or grandmother did.

I thought we were neglecting them and turning them all into homosexuals.

Definitely not. Women today spend more time doing things like child care.

If you need proof of how tranquil the relations between the sexes have become, look at what's happened to the two former generalissimos of chauvinism, Mickey Spillane and Norman Mailer. Mailer's into writing apologetic articles for ladies' magazines and Spillane's become a booster for monogamy — a mellowed, soft-spoken charmer. Spillane earned fame and fortune living and writing about a lifestyle that I've always despised. Yet was I hostile when I met him? Not at all. His views on women are so hopelessly irrelevant

that I actually found myself nostalgic. That's how little com-
bat is left in me. As for Mickey, he hasn't got much else that's
preoccupying him these days besides home and fishing.
While standing around the office waiting to be interviewed,
he talked of oysters, his house on the ocean, and the joys of
his decade-old marriage to Sherri. Four months after this
interview was broadcast, Sherri — the object of Spillane's
ardour — walked out. I actually felt sad for him.

How did you meet Sherri, Mickey?
> You really wanna know how I met my wife? We needed a
> girl for the cover of my book. I said, "Send us over a
> blonde with beautiful dancer's legs, the kind I like —
> those nice, round, big legs — you know." I told 'em I
> don't care if she looks like a dog because we're not going
> to show her face. So they sent Sherri over, and I never
> sent her back. For two hours we did all this rolling
> around, from kissing to whatever, and the guy only shot
> two rolls of film. I paid him just to keep the camera
> going.

Do you still think women love rough treatment?
> Nah — with a woman you punch 'em right in the mouth
> with your lips — that quiets them down. No, my wife likes
> the way I work with her. She always wins when I punch
> her in the mouth — come here, honey. Works, too. Costs
> me a lot of money, but it comes off pretty good.

So you've changed, too?
> Yeah, but I never believed in this Women's Lib business.
> You know, there are ways you treat women. And don't
> think that women don't know how to treat you, too. Boy,
> they're the slickest things around. Like my wife says to
> me: "Don't ever liberate me from my fur coat and my
> diamond ring. I like it this way."

People are going to picket her nightclub act if you keep
quoting her this way.
> Well, I like women the way they're supposed to be.

You and Norman Mailer have the same taste, I think.
> Yeah, women.

But you have a certain kind of woman you like.
> Yeah, beautiful blondes. It costs my wife — what is it —

sixty bucks every other week to be a beautiful blonde. Terrible. She's going to kill me.

She is. And you deserve it.

Well, have you ever seen a real blonde outside of Sweden? You see a blonde walking down a street, you know it's a phoney.

So why do you like it?

I don't know. There's something pretty nice about that. Like Mike Hammer looked at this girl one day and said, "My beautiful blonde has a brunette base, but that makes her all the more interesting."

Don't you believe in anything else?

Well, you know I'm kind of old-fashioned. If a woman would let a guy take care of her and be a woman everything would be fine. But when they run out and start making the decisions and doing everything else, they turn the men into mice, which is stupid. You know, if I were a woman and my husband stayed out later and later every night, I'd go up and take a nice bath, kick all the kids out, and meet him at the door dressed in something — maybe undressed in something, who knows. So when he knocks on the door, walks in — wow, there you are — whoom, great time. Boy, he won't be staying out late.

Has it ever worried you that maybe it's your wife's backside selling the books instead of your words?

What kills me is that she's doing a show for three months now, doing this crazy dance routine, and she worked her tail off. She hasn't got that beautiful *tuchus* like she used to have before. Now I've got to get her back on the cheesecake routine and build her back up the way I like her. I want a nice, round — oooh — you know what I mean.

Once it was only celebrities who got divorced; the rest of us were supposed to stay together. Now just about everybody I know seems to be cooly walking out of marriage, working through lawyers to settle who gets the sofa, who gets the vacuum cleaner, and when the kids will visit. For those wives who feel wounded and vindictive, there's even a feminist newspaper in New York that will publish a character assassination of their particular enemy.

Malcolm Muggeridge is not so much *for* marriage, I suspect, as he is *against* divorce – especially when it's over "piffling little difficulties" like sexual incompatibility. Whenever Muggeridge comes to Toronto, I like to talk to him. Usually we concentrate on Jesus, but this time I managed to divert him for a moment – although just barely – onto hostility between the sexes.

Why is there so much divorce lately, Mr. Muggeridge?

> Well, it's part of the collapse of Christianity, of course, because if people join themselves together, a man and a woman, primarily to achieve mutual erotic satisfaction, then that will be a very limited pursuit – as everybody who's had any experience of such things knows. If, on the other hand, they join themselves together in love to make a family, which is the small unit of the larger family of God, then they won't wish to separate simply because some piffling little difficulties have arisen.

Piffling little difficulties?

> About their miserable sex life, or something like that. Which is utterly unimportant compared with the larger purpose.

But people would argue that we only go around once –

> I don't know what that means, quite.

That means they don't expect to have a sex life in heaven so they want one on Earth, because someone's told them they're entitled to it.

> It's such a miserable little pursuit in itself that I simply can't sort of – I mean I can't –

You didn't always feel that way, I bet.

> I never in my life believed that sex in itself is a *sine qua non* of living. I mean, it would be like saying that having a filet mignon every day is the *sine qua non*. Meat eaters may find having a filet mignon a very grand experience and I wouldn't take it from them. But if you're going to come snivelling up to me and say that if I can't have a filet mignon in heaven I must have five now – well, God help you.

An awful lot of good people are breaking out of marriage.
   Certainly.
And abandoning their children to the other spouse.
   I pity them so much. I not only pity them, but I feel great
   sympathy with them because they've been misled.
   They've been brainwashed by all the fatuous nonsense.
The assumption that marriage must always be serene?
   That it must be perfect, that the minute it becomes
   troubled, they're entitled, quite irresponsibly and with-
   out reference to anybody else, to embark upon another.
What does your wife say?
   You know, we shall celebrate our golden wedding if we
   live to 1977. We've lived together for half a century and
   we understand each other.
Is your wife just tolerant, maybe?
   She is a very delightful person. I know she is, but the
   point is that what destroys marriages is not infidelities,
   not quarrelling. What destroys marriages is the imbecile
   belief that two human beings, two frail mortal human
   beings, bound together in this very curious relationship,
   which has to begin in physical terms, can create together
   a perfectly serene and peaceful time; and if and when it
   ceases to be so they must slam the door, leave their
   children, and pack the whole thing up. This is the absur-
   dity.

   There was a lovely, naive idea around in the middle
sixties that when women were finally equal, everybody
would be better for it. Aggression would end, co-operation
would replace coercion, and human goodness would at last
prevail. Of course, it was self-delusion and chauvinism of
another sort to think that God appointed woman His custo-
dian of all the finer virtues. Not only can women be just as
beastly, alcoholic, criminal, and competitive, they also
make obscene phone calls. John Ferguson, who works for
the telephone company in Philadelphia, told us about it.

How do you know women are making more obscene calls,
Mr. Ferguson?

Well, I'll tell you this. Five years ago, when I first took this job, it would be so unusual to hear somebody complaining about a woman using obscene language on the phone that everybody would pass it around the office. It was a little hee-haw. But that's no longer the case. It's no longer an unusual call.

What do the women say on their obscene calls?

Oh, we don't listen to them, Ma'am. That is against the law.

Well, are they deep breathers or swearers?

They get into both. But we consider breathing only a harassing call. It's not obscene unless they start to get suggestive. Actually, women have always been very big in the field of deep breathing. This is the triangle type of thing. The husband is running around, so you call his girlfriend and either breathe hard to scare her, or you just hang up and hang up and hang up to harass her. That's been done for years by females. What's new is the obscenity.

Is there a classic pattern that the obscene caller starts off with?

They've got to get you listening to their spiel and when they get you hooked, they'll come along and zing you with their obscene remarks. One of the famous ones down here was a fellow — we call him the bra salesman — who claimed he worked for a lingerie company and he was giving away free lingerie, but he had to have all the sizes before he could send you this package. So he would ask the woman the size of her bra and pants and her slip and everything else, and he would get more and more suggestive as to the type of brand. Before they knew it, they were into an obscene call and didn't realize it, because these fellows are slick, they're good at it. This is their hobby and they're as good at this as a stamp collector is at collecting stamps.

What do the women callers do, sell jockey shorts?

Well, they haven't used that. They'll call up and they'll say, "Hi, big boy," and "Would you like to talk a little dirty with me for a while?" And the average guy does. That's why we don't begin to get reports of all the cases where this happens. An average case is a guy sitting home alone while his wife's out shopping, and some girl calls him and they talk obscene for thirty minutes. This guy doesn't want his wife to know he's received a call, because the first question is going to be, why didn't you hang up? So these women get away with it.

If only you could hook up these obscene women to the obscene men.

Yeah, we've thought about that, Barbara, for a long time. Hooking the two of them together in some way. That way they wouldn't bother anybody else, you know. They could spend all day dialling and that would take care of our problem.

You might even get some marriages out of it.

Yeah, if there are some marriages made in heaven, why not some made in the phone booth?

When Masters and Johnson confirmed in their laboratories that women's capacity for sexual pleasure was certainly equal to and possibly superior to men's, male supremacists took those findings as one more assault in the war between the sexes. "Anything you can do, I can do better" is not a song that Romeos want to hear in bed. It didn't take long for the counterattack. Paul Cameron, Associate Professor of Human Development at St. Mary's College, Maryland, wasn't at all impressed by the fact that women could do it. The question for him was: did they enjoy it? The results of Cameron's survey offered threatened males the first good news they've had since Kinsey. For men, it seems, sex remains the *numero uno* activity. For women, it rates only fifth — after housework, just ahead of smoking.

Okay, Dr. Cameron, let's hear the results.

Fine. We found that for females, sex never got higher than fifth in the rating, and that was only attained by women ages eighteen through twenty-five. After that, it dropped rather precipitously. Females claimed greater pleasure from music, nature, being with their families, and travelling, than they did from sexual activity. For males, on the other hand, from the age of sixteen through the middle forties, they ranked sex number one, or rather it turned up number one in their ratings.

But you men brag, don't forget. Women are a little more modest. So a lot of men might rate sex number one even if they like music better, too. Or housework or sports.

What you are saying is true, especially for middle-aged and older respondents. On the other hand, I think the magnitude of difference between the responses of men and women is too great to write them off that simply. I think it could be argued, for example, that males have many more reasons to enjoy sex than females. Look at what a man gets out of sex. It's a point scored. If you do a good job, you have something to be very pleased about and maybe even to brag about.

Fine. But —

Generally speaking, the sheer biological pleasure associated with climaxing would be about the same, of course, for the two sexes.

They rate the same on the Richter scale?

Probably so. Every once in a while you'll run into a female who can just volley till you're blue in the face, and you say, "Gee whiz, that must be super." But there are plenty of females who have a hell of a time climaxing at all. And given that, even the poorest male can manage something for himself, even if he can't please his female partner.

Ah — now, aren't we getting to a crucial part of the business? Could we be talking about selfish men and not sexually uninterested women?

Well, I don't know. I'm sure there's a large number of poorly trained or prepared sex partners.

And couldn't that account for why fewer women rate sex number one? That they've got lousy lovers at home with them?

Well, then again, one could say that they're terribly hard to please. It depends which way you come at it. It's the man who has the onus of doing a good job, not the woman. The woman, if she allows the man or permits him, has fulfilled 90 per cent of what she's supposed to do; it's the man who has to do whatever else is required.

The women over forty — what did they rate ahead of sex?
What kind of things?

> Just about everything but the kitchen sink. About the
> only thing they didn't rate above sex was smoking, drink-
> ing alcohol, and — let's see, what else —

So they like housework more?

> Housework higher by a long shot.

Church work?

> Church higher also, right. Again, women didn't say that
> they didn't enjoy sex, just that they enjoyed it to a much
> more moderate degree than males did. Males are rather
> the frantic ones about the thing. That's why they are
> continually in amazement that females treat this — the
> most sacred of all their subjects — so casually, so disin-
> terestedly.

Even in a phoney war there are bound to be a lot of
casualties. Geza Hornyak of Hamilton, Ontario, is one of
them. Hornyak came to Canada from Hungary twenty years
ago and, having made a small success of himself, thought he
should find a wife and settle down — not an extravagant
ambition. But, as they will, the fates conspired. Three times
in three years poor Hornyak found himself ditched by his
young Hungarian brides, who'd only married him to confirm
their landed immigrant status — the very kind of selfish stunt
that men have often pulled on women.

Mr. Hornyak, you haven't been very lucky, have you?

> Not lately. Not in the past three years.

Let's start at the beginning. What was your goal?

> Well, I'm twenty years here and I've had a little bit of
> luck in this country. I was working hard for it, though.
> And I thought it's about time to get married and settle
> down, you know, in this age. That was my goal.

You never got married in Canada all these years?

> I was married to a Canadian girl once but that marriage
> don't work out. So I decided maybe I better off if I
> looking for a same nationality like I am. You know, I am
> Hungarian.

Has it been the same story with all three girls?

Same story with all three girls. The first girl, I married her in 1971. After, I found out that she was out here visiting and her passport is expired so she needed somebody to marry her. That way she could stay in the country.

Did she explain that to you, that she was using you for a meal ticket?

She didn't explain anything. Before the marriage everything was fine — promises and everything. And the first day of the marriage, nothing. The marriage was broke up on the very first day. I didn't even get a divorce from her. I got an annulment.

These girls must have been terrific actresses. How did you go for it? Are you so naive?

No. I am not naive. I have quite experience, but maybe I was blind because I just jumped into it too quick. And she was a con-artist. She was doing everything, anything. There was nothing I couldn't ask from her she wouldn't do it, and after the first day — right on the very first day, right on the wedding day — she almost told to me like I got nothing to do with you. We went out to a nice big dinner, we had a few drinks, we took some pictures with the wedding.

All at your expense?

All at my expense, naturally. And after the time came, okay, we are man and wife, we returned to — well, what I would say, to the honeymoon night. And she said, "No way, you're not going to sleep with me, you know."

That must have shocked you.

That was really a shock to me. And then, just like a bomb dropped, I knew I was a sucker.

And all three played you the same way?

Approximately like that, yes.

How come you didn't learn from your first two mistakes? On the third, why weren't you more suspicious?

Well, because I thought, you know, every bushel has a bad apple, and I never thought. Well, everybody can't be the same.

Your bushel's had three.

I had three because I digged in three different bushels.

What have these romances cost you in total?

Oh, in total it cost me at least six thousand dollars.

Quite a bundle.

Which I don't care about. I would have given ten thousand dollars if even one of them would have stayed with me and I was happily married — because I was in love with the girls, you know.

What kind of husband were you, Mr. Hornyak? Maybe you've got to look at yourself a bit.

How could I answer that question? Because if I say I would be a wonderful husband or I was a wonderful husband, naturally everybody thinks, "Well, he's talking, he's pushing his own story."

But maybe you come on too strong or maybe you're too demanding about the cooking?

No. No. No. As a matter of fact I think my problem is that I'm really soft. I really show them right from the first I love them and I didn't ask anything to do. As a matter of fact I help them. I do the washing. I do the ironing. I wash the kitchen floor. Because I do like to have somebody in the house when I come home. It's not enough if you have a little bit of money in the bank. You've got to have a place to go to come home. It's not a home without a woman.

Now that there seems to be a kind of truce between the sexes, there are very few men around who'll risk promoting new hostilities by suggesting that women ought to know their place. That puts a special burden then on traditionalists like Stan Obodiac, outspoken publicist for the Toronto Maple Leafs. Obodiac knows where women belong, and it's not in the dressing rooms of his beloved Leafs. When female sportswriters demanded equal journalistic opportunity in that male sanctuary, Obodiac defied them in the name of decency. With such a cause, how could I deny him the last word on this subject?

Are you ready for women in your dressing rooms, Mr. Obodiac?

No, I'm definitely not ready for them at all.

How about the players?

Well, I don't think the players are, either, because I see this as a corruption of our morals that has been going on for the last ten years.

What morals?

The morals of society, the morals of society in general. And don't say, "Who says so?" I says so. And any right-thinking individual says so, too. You get that sort of opinion from the teachers of morality right down through history and you better carry on with that, because when you see corruption in society, you see the end of the world in sight.

How does all this relate to journalists in the dressing room?

Well it's just part of it, you see. A decent woman — excuse me if I use that term — wouldn't think of going into the Leafs' dressing room. I'm not aware of certain other customs in other parts of the world. I know that in the South Pacific women walk around, say, nude to the waist all over, and that means into every type of men's habitation. But that is not the custom in Western society, so —

But I'm not sure why you object, Mr. Obodiac. If the women are not in it for prurient reasons, and surely no serious journalist would be, what's wrong with it?

For one thing, you are going to get a feedback from the player's wives. Certainly they don't want these women associating with the men in the nude, you know. It's going to create a difficult situation at home, so let's stop the situation.

What do you think the wives would worry about?

They're worried about, say, some of these women possibly seeing more of their husbands than they do.

That's pretty frightening.

It's not frightening. After all, they are busy. But this is a possibility.

Then again, players are kind of exhibitionistic, aren't they?

No, they're not.

They're not?

They're not exhibitionists at all, no.

They never touch each other?

No — absolutely. They might hit somebody over the head or something like that. After all, if they win, they're just tremendously exuberant. So you may see some of this fondling out on the ice. It may even continue into the dressing room, where somebody whacks somebody a compliment for a good game. But that's all — well, that's normal between all human beings.

It's the beginning of the end, Mr. Obodiac. You know that, don't you? The locker room's about to fall.

No, it won't fall. You see, we've already anticipated this. We've built a little side room where you'll be able to see the coaches and where we can bring out the players in suitable attire. So, you see, at Maple Leaf Gardens we're always working in advance of the mores of society.

Mr. Obodiac, thanks a lot. Thanks for fighting for morals.

I'm fighting for more than that. I'm fighting for civilization itself.

Eight
Funny People . . . Funny Odd and Funny Haw-Haw

Whether Walter "The Great" Cornelius was having me on – and in the process sending up every daredevil who's ever lurched at fame – or whether he was simply the most lovable kook I've ever talked to, I've never quite decided. Walter's bid for notoriety started with a small want ad in his local English newspaper, seeking twenty strongmen for a stunt that would dwarf the exploits of the greatest daredevils, from Houdini to Knievel. Cornelius needed the strongmen to pull back on a giant rubberband slingshot that he'd designed to hurl him across a nearby river and onto the front page of every newspaper in the world.

It sounded terrific. And The Great Cornelius did not let us down. We dialled his number in Peterborough, England, and gladly waited a few moments while his wife went to fetch him from the pub next door. I hunched that we were in for some laughs as soon as the shouting Dutchman panted onto the line, out of his noggin with excitement that Canada thought him worthy of a trans-Atlantic phone call.

There you are, Mr. Cornelius. We're calling from Canada. Can you hear me?

Yes, I can hear you. I've just run out of breath –
Take your time, take it easy. Are you sure you're in good enough condition for this stunt you're planning?

Yes – what do you expect? I've just run four miles, you know that? I chased around four miles because I'm slimming.

That's funny. Your wife told us you were out for a beer. But never mind. Tell us about this stunt you're going to do with the rubberbands.

It's not with rubberbands. I'm going to do it *mit* catapult.

Like a slingshot and you're the stone?

That's it.

And these twenty strongmen are going to drag you back in this rubber slingshot and let go and you're going to go zinging across the river?

That's the one. These men pull me down and then you let her go and it shoots off.

And away you go?

Yes.

How far are you going to try and go?

Three hundred yards, Madame, maybe further out.

Mr. Cornelius, this trick with the catapult, is it dangerous? Are you risking your life?

Oh, yes, most indeed. I'm risking ever so much my life. Because, you see, I don't know how I can land at the other side. I don't know whether I can reach that net, whether I cannot reach. Oh, yes, I risk my life.

Have you done other stunts like this?

In 1970 I jumped off the roof of a supermarket.

You didn't hurt yourself, I hope.

Oh, yes, I did. I broke it five teeth, broken nose and joint. You know "cracked a joint," yes?

Why didn't you glide down on something like a parachute?

Nah – I don't believe in that. If you're going down, you're going down.

What was your all-time best?

Best stunt last year. Won the world's strongest man. Won in Japan.

What did you have to do to win that?

See, I am a strongman for start. And while I'm not young – I'm about fifty-four years old – I've been doing these stunts and I've always got good ideas for that. I pull two double-decker buses *mit* my teeth, four people sitting in. Two double-decker bus I pull with my teeth seven hundred yards in Japan.

Wow.

　　And then I lift a car *mit* my legs and arms and four men sitting in. Oh, yes, listen — I am the strongest man in the world. I hold thirty-one world records. I even entered world champion sausage-eating a couple of months ago, before a Japanese beat me. One of these sumo wrestlers. He won. He ate more than I did.

How many sausages did you eat?

　　I ate it four and a half pounds in eight minutes, and this Japanese, he ate five and a half in six minutes.

Are you in training now? Are you laying off beer?

　　I'm doing most on diet. Lots of raw meat, raw eggs. And I eat a lot of grass.

You're kidding.

　　I'm not.

You're putting this whole thing on. How do you eat raw grass?

　　Just like horse eat grass, cow eat grass, so I am. Why not? Nice and tasty, you know. Put a bit of pepper *und* salt, it's nice, tasty.

Who cuts the grass for you?

　　The children, you know, small children.

Mr. Cornelius, you're giving our producers here a stroke.

　　What you mean, there's people listening? Say hello to everybody.

What do you look like, Walter?

　　How I look? You know John Wayne? He's American film star, John Wayne.

Yeah.

　　I look exactly — if you put the two photographs together, John Wayne and me, you wouldn't know which is which.

Good luck to you, Walter.

　　Thanks so much. Nice to talk with you. Listen — if I do it, can you call me again?

You bet your life.

　　What Cornelius has figured out is that oddness sells — it always has. All you need is a gimmick. Abbie Hoffman and Jerry Rubin combined craziness with politics and scored heavily in the sixties. Comedians from Charlie Chaplin to Mel Brooks have made fortunes pretending to be weird. Mel Brooks began as a comedy writer for people like Sid Caesar, but he now saves his best lines for himself. His 2,000-year-old man and his Yiddish-speaking Indian chief from *Blazing Saddles* are two great comic inventions. I had a chance to play straightperson to Mel Brooks when he was flying high after the release of *Blazing Saddles*, and this was the result.

Mr. Brooks, why is God being so good to you lately?

> God is being good to me because I am fervently religious, because every morning I crash to my knees and I pray. I have joined with some people called Purples. Everything is purple except their navels. The navel is a beautiful flesh tone. But all the rest of them is completely purple, and it's wonderful. All we ask for is grain. We live for grain — rolled oats, whole wheat, and wheat germ.

Do you ever wonder what you'd be doing if you had married a Jewish princess?

> If I'd married a Jewish princess instead of my wonderful Italian wife? I probably would be selling opals. I would have 10,000 opals in a big lot in Santa Ana, California. That's what I'd be doing, because a Jewish princess needs a ring on every finger.

You'd better tell everybody what a Jewish princess is.

> A Jewish princess is a girl who is born into a Jewish family and who never puts her hand in dish water. She is born not to work and she grows very long nails like the Chinese in the eleventh century, to prove that she's never worked, because with long nails you can't work. And they get presents. When they're born they get a diamond heart that replaces their own heart of flesh for the rest of their lives.

Mr. Brooks, which part of the movie do you like best — the acting, the producing, the casting — do you like casting?

> I like casting. Show us your legs, Freddie.

That was bad taste, Mr. Brooks.

> Yeah, I think so. I revel in bad taste, because in good taste you might as well work in a matzo factory. Bad taste

is simply saying the truth, before it should be said, maybe. Don't you think that after seeing 10,000 movies showing cowboys eating beans, it was about time somebody did a picture where they let a couple go? I mean, let the shoe drop, let the other shoe drop. You can't drink black coffee and beans and ride horses and not let there be wind across the prairie.

Are all the taboos gone?

Yes. As a matter of fact, ten years from now you will see filth on the TV screen, absolute filth. People will be doing it in your living room. Jewish mothers will faint in front of the screen. There will be mayhem going on.

Will it be Mel Brooks doing the filth?

No, no. I'm clean as a whistle. No dirt on me, lady. I don't like it. I don't even do it with people with wives, you know.

Mr. Brooks, are you normal?

I am normal, yes. I am normal. You will see me standing up at urinals. You will see me sitting down on the little seat. I mean, I do whatever anybody does that's normal. I will say, "Waitress, another cup of coffee, please, when you have time." I'm very normal.

Mr. Brooks, are you a good husband?

I'm a one-woman man. I'm not sure which woman, you know, but whoever she is I'm a one-woman guy. Who needs those phone calls? "The Indiana Motel?" "The funny woman with the big wart that brought the towels?" Who wants those calls on the telephone? I don't want them. Therefore I am very faithful because I don't need people calling me later.

Thank you, Mr. Brooks.

Barbara, it's been a pleasure eating up your air time. And please tender my regards to all the citizens of Canada. Tell them that they all sound like Randolph Scott. They do not say "house" or "mouse," they say "hoose" or "moose." I love it. And I think they are taller than Americans, they are kinder, and they are more gentle. I'm serious. I think they make time for you. All my pictures for some reason do sensationally in Canada. Now, what I'm after in Canada is the Mountie. I must liberate the Mountie. He is frigid. The Mountie doesn't do it. We must allow the Mountie to do it twice before he dies. That is my main purpose, my drive in life, to get that Mountie. I want every Mountie to be like Carman Miranda — fruit on his head, moving around, swivel those hips. Do what God intended you to do, not just grab your holster and look to the sun.

The *Guinness Book of Records* now needs over 300 pages to keep track of all the people who are willing to give us some laughs in order to earn themselves some fame and glory. But, let me tell you, there are tens of thousands more who are anxious to play at oddness for the most paltry media attention. Jimmy Artis of Chicago wanted to be noticed so badly that he went to court to change his name to Adolph Hitler. Another guy I spoke with married his horse. The California gentleman who bills himself as The World's Biggest Eater, Edward "Bozo" Miller, is a good example of the type, a man who has taken a bad food habit and turned it into show-business.

What have you eaten today, Bozo?

Today? I had a fairly good breakfast, maybe a dozen eggs, half a dozen English muffins, twelve strips of bacon. Then around 8:30 I had a few donuts. At noon I went to lunch and I had eight or nine martinis, then sat down and had three steak sandwiches and the vegetables that go with them. Some banana shortcake for dessert, two bottles of wine, and some cordials after. Then around 3:30 we stopped at another saloon and had a few more drinks.

How do you work it off? Do you go jogging every morning?

Oh no, no, no. I used to work out, but I'm getting too old to work out now. It's too hard. I'm getting on.

How old are you?

I'll be sixty-seven this June.

The Guinness people say that no one's been able to out-eat you since 1931. What records do you hold?

I still hold twenty-seven chickens in a few hours. And the raviolis, about 250 in one hour.

How do you know when you're full?

Well, you're stuffed, you're full. There's no reason to force yourself. I'm just eating for pleasure and drinking for pleasure.

Is this talent or is this training?

I've always been a large eater, but I say that when you have to eat more, you have to train. Your stomach is just so large and you have to enlarge it. I ate a whole prime rib once, I think it weighed twenty-seven pounds. I'd say that was the hardest thing I ever had to eat.

Why was that so hard?

Because you have to chew it.

If we wanted to, we could showcase a character like Bozo Miller every night. And usually we want to, for this simple reason: people relate to crazies. I'm never told our coverage of Lebanon was super; it's always, "Hey, that King Kong guy crying in the phone booth in Chicago — what an item!" Besides, who says Cod Wars or deficit Olympic spending are any less absurd? Kooks, at least, are fun. And they're always easy to talk to. You just go for details, question plainly, keep your distance, and — above all — hold the judgments. The stuntman who keeps blowing his broken body skyward with dynamite to satisfy the lust of a paying crowd can live without my lay analysis of his motives. And Bozo the trencherman, who consumes 25,000 calories a day to maintain his Guinness girth, does not require my pity or my views on gluttony.

Rules like those, of course, are made to be broken. Every once in a while the comedian puts on his other face. That's what happened the night we came upon a Florida taxi driver named Mike Aprile. Aprile was also trying to live off gluttony — another bit player in our nightly parade of newsmakers. He came to us billed as a spaghetti champ, with aspirations to the ravioli crown as well.

This time I thought I'd do a how-to-do-it story — the eating secrets of a fat man willing to choke down a sinkful of pasta at one go. I started in my usual way. But from his first snuffled words it was clear that Aprile was in agony. Obviously, this was quite a different kind of story. Exploit your freakiness and I'll go with it. Play the clown and I am there with all the necessary applause. But start sinking in remorse and self-hatred in the middle of the interview; weigh 370 pounds as Aprile did and then foul up your last chance at the obesity clinic by making a pig of yourself at a spaghetti marathon — and Barbara Frum, bleeding heart, must wade in to save you.

How long did it take you to eat the spaghetti, Mr. Aprile?
> Ninety minutes.
And you ate how much spaghetti?
> Six pounds and thirteen and three-quarter ounces. Just
> a few forks shy of seven dishes.
Were the other contestants professional spaghetti eaters or just out for a lark?
> None of them was professionals. It doesn't take a profes-
> sional to do that. In fact, one guy almost beat me, but he
> didn't last. He lost his — he got disqualified for you-
> know-what.
No, for what?
> Heaving.
What's the extra ingredient you bring to a contest? What makes a champ?
> Well, you can't sit down and eat it real fast. You gotta eat
> it slow, cut it up, chop it up, pack it tight in your mouth.
> Get all the juice out of it. Get it real tight and then
> swallow it. Pack it like snuff and then swallow it. Do it
> slow and use a little sauce because the starch in the
> spaghetti will get you nauseated after a while just tasting
> it.
How do you get rid of the excess liquid? Are you allowed to drool?
> No, but when nobody is looking you kind of — you gotta
> spit between your teeth to get rid of that juice. Another

little trick I use is working my stomach muscles the whole time, pushing it with my hand.

How does that help?

It works your stomach, works your digestive system a little bit — makes it go.

You know, it's great talking to you, Mr. Aprile, because most people who win contests never tell us the trade.

I don't care . . . because I'm not gonna be in this much longer . . . because my psychiatrist and my therapist are really upset. I promised them I wouldn't eat. I told them I was going up there to be a judge. . . . Now it's in all the newspapers. I don't want to be spaghetti champion. I want to get well. . . . I keep disappointing them, and they keep hanging in there with me because they really care about me and love me. . . . What's hurting me is hurting them, because they really care about me. That's what's got me upset, hurting them —

I really can see that.

I mean it. I love them and they love me but I've really disappointed them this time — again, you know. It's bothering me real bad. I feel like just shooting myself.

Mr. Aprile, I really know what you feel like. You've just got to like yourself more.

That's what the people at the hospital want me to do, my doctor and all them. I sure don't like myself when I get myself into something like this.

You just have to stop hating yourself.

I told the promoters I wasn't going to eat and they said just eat one bowl — get the people there — and that's it. But then all them people around there bet money on me. That's what drove me, because I wasn't going to let them down, all the people who bet money on me because of my big mouth around there, promoting that thing. I forced myself from the first bite to the last.

Well, you get back to your doctor and get down to 190 or so and you're going to love yourself.

Yeah, then I can write a book and get rich off the book. I don't need any spaghetti contests. I'm not going to humiliate myself or lower my dignity for peanuts.

That's right. That's right. Would you like cards of encouragement?

Sure, I'd appreciate that.

People like Mike Aprile and Bozo Miller do an important job for the rest of us. They've taken the place of the sideshow freaks who used to comfort us with their grotesqueness. Now that authentic freaks are few and far between, all those reassuring things that we relied on funny-looking people to do for us — make us feel less ugly, less fat, less hairy, less stupid — must be done by these self-invented types. They pay a terrible price for it, of course. Because in that very moment when we are identifying with their pain and their hunger for acceptance, in that same instant we are also repulsed by them. I have always found that ambivalence intriguing. So does Leslie Fiedler, the distinguished American literary critic. He's been thinking and writing about freaks for a long time now, concentrating on the freaks that God has created, rather than the self-made variety.

I'm so interested that you are interested in freaks, too, Mr. Fiedler. How do you account for our fascination?

I've discovered that understanding what freaks mean to me turns out to be an exploration of my own psyche. I've always been interested in marginal people, you know. I've written a lot about American Indians, about black people, about Jews, but it seems to me that the people who stand on the last margins of what we define as human are the freaks. They represent the kind of total indignity of people who are excluded. Right now I'm interested in classic freaks, the kind of people who have been shown at fairs or regarded with a mixture of religious horror and admiration — dwarfs, giants, hermaphrodites, siamese twins, human skeletons, fat men, fat ladies, and so forth.

Are you also interested in what it does to them to be a freak?

Yes, I am. For instance, why is it that in the late twentieth century, when the natural human anomalies are beginning to organize, rejecting the name "freak" and asking to be called by other names – no longer wanting to be thought of as freaks – there is a large part of the population who would ordinarily be taken as normal, but who designate themselves as freaks?

I didn't realize that there were movements to rehabilitate the image of freaks.

Oh, yes. The first group to organize were the dwarfs, who in some ways are the aristocrats of the freaks. One of the groups that Hitler tried to eliminate completely were the midgets. Maybe that's one of the reasons why their organization is especially strong.

And yet you called them the "aristocrats." What makes them that?

In the history of freakdom, they are the people who are best known. We know the names of distinguished dwarfs going all the way back to ancient Egypt. Do you know freaks have been advisers to kings and have been kings and emperors themselves? For instance, they boast that Attila the Hun was a midget. And there have been other midget rulers. The midgets have a history of having been brought into the courts of Europe as entertainers and performing fools, sort of human pets, and working their way up into positions as advisers and state counsellors. The last instance of that is that Nasser had a dwarf as his confidante. This tradition has not died in the Middle East.

And yet we're so afraid of them, too, aren't we?

We're afraid of them. We wonder at them. People swing back and forth on this, thinking that freaks are so uncanny that they should be killed at birth. They're a kind of taboo human being because they call into question all of our definitions of what it is to be human. When one looks at a dwarf, for instance, what's called into question is the difference between a child and a grown-up. And when we look at an hermaphrodite, it is the polar distinction we make between the sexes. Then there are the freaks who had names like Lionel the Lion-Faced Boy, or Joe-Joe the Dog-Faced Boy. These are people who make you think about the line we draw between lower animals and human beings.

It gets into that stuff about "made in God's image."

Yeah, right. I mean, if you think about a man who has been made in God's image having two eyes and one nose, what do you do about a man who has one eye and two noses?

Some of it surely is just aesthetic. It's just so unhappy-making to look at someone who looks so miserable.

But, on the other hand, it's more complicated than that, because it turns out that most freaks lead fairly happy and well-adjusted lives. They get married. They have children. They're often wooed. A woman who was shown as the Mule Woman, who was reported to have been the ugliest woman who ever lived – hair growing all over her face, with distorted features and so forth – was wooed all her life and married three times.

How do you account for that?

The same thing that repels people also attracts them. One wants to possess that somehow. I think there's a terrible ambivalence about the whole thing. I've never met anybody who didn't have a freak story to tell and who wasn't eager to listen to one.

My favourite, lately, is the man who had to decide whether to undergo surgery that would repair his terrible facial scarring and make him unemployable as a freak. That fascinates me – the struggle about whether or not to go straight.

In a recent case of siamese twins, an operation was done with great difficulty to make these people able to live separate lives. But Chang and Eng, the original siamese twins, lived an immensely successful life; they married two sisters and had sixteen children between them. They ran a successful farm and they actually owned slaves.

Wow. Were they back to back? I assume they were.

They were connected by a kind of thick ligature that ran from chest to chest, but by long practice and stretching they got so that they could face away from each other.

It still doesn't make for a lot of privacy.

No, it doesn't indeed. That's one of the things that intrigues people. There's something erotic about freaks,

I think. Everybody worries about the sex lives of siamese twins, for example, but apparently it all works out somehow.

Things hadn't been working out for The World's Tallest Girl when I first met her. Her life had been pretty miserable, in fact, which is probably why she finally found the nerve to exploit her freakiness and try to make it pay. When I asked her why she'd gone out of her way to call public attention to her extraordinary dimensions, she was perfectly blunt about it. As she figured it, the exposure might not reconcile her to her situation, but enough invitations to appear at shopping-centre and supermarket openings might at least let her buy an outsized car. Sandy Allen was only nineteen when she did this interview. She was seven feet and five inches tall and weighed 420 pounds.

Hi, Miss Allen. I'm just looking at a picture of you in the newspaper.
    Oh, my goodness, they even ran a picture!
How are you enjoying your new fame?
    I'm really enjoying it. I've got calls from all over the place — Detroit, Miami, New York, California, Boston — every place.
What do they want?
    Oh, they ask me what my problems are, what the disadvantages are of being tall. And if I have any plans made for the future, as far as my height is concerned — my life's ambition or whatever.
Why did you get in touch with the Guinness people?
    Well, I've had nothing but a lot of wisecracks all my life. So one day I called the state library in Indianapolis and asked them to look in the Guinness book for me and see how tall the tallest living woman was. I found out she was only seven feet, five inches tall, and I am slightly more. So I wrote a letter to London and told them about myself. They wrote back telling me that they didn't know of any other woman who could claim to be my height and that

they would send me an official certificate stating that I was the tallest.

But why did you bother?

Well, like I say, all I've had all my life is a lot of wise-cracks and I really would like to make something of it now.

Like what?

Money.

Trying to make an asset of a liability.

Right. You're right there, that's for sure.

How do you react when people point at you? I can imagine that little kids might even be scared.

They are rather amazed, you know. They just don't know what to say — "Mommy, look at that big girl." They don't realize what they are saying. But when adults stand and laugh at me, then is when it hurts. I don't mind people staring at me, because I imagine if I was of normal height and I saw someone my size I'd have to stare, too. But when they just stand there and laugh, it kind of upsets me. I've just learned to consider the source and go on.

It must be very hard to have friends.

With my female friends there's no trouble. But as far as the opposite sex is concerned, I'm afraid I haven't had very many dates in my life.

You should meet the world's tallest man.

I'm going to before long. I've been talking to him.

Does he sound like a decent person?

Oh, he's really nice. I really liked him, the way he sounded.

Is he single?

Yes, he's single. I think he's about forty-eight or forty-nine.

So it sounds like he's had the same kind of problems.

I imagine so. We are intending to get together and talk over a few things.

Make fun of the little people?

That's right.

As rare and marvellous as living freaks can be, dead freaks are even more so. That's why the University of Montreal's medical museum won't part with the body of Edward Beaupré, the Giant of Willowbunch, whose family dearly wants to bring him home to Saskatchewan for burial. Beaupré has been on view in Montreal for over sixty years. He lies there in his glass box – all eight feet, three inches and 375 pounds of him – the showpiece of the museum. That ghoulish exploitation bothers and revolts me.

The story of the giant had begun for us as a piece of nationalistic trivia, at a time when we were all scurrying after characters to colour our collective past. Beaupré was perfect: Canada's very own giant, one of the biggest men who'd ever lived. He was born in 1881, the oldest of twenty children, a shy fellow and a good cowboy, until he had to give up riding because his feet kept dragging on the ground. When they could no longer afford to clothe him, Beaupré's parents sent him off with a travelling circus. Five years later he was dead of tuberculosis; but Beaupré, now embalmed, continued on in show business. He toured North America for a few more seasons, until a crate containing his body was left behind in Montreal. For the price of the storage charges, the university museum got itself a centrepiece.

It was fifty years after that, with poor Beaupré still on display at the University of Montreal, that the family in Willowbunch finally caught up with their benighted relative. This is the interview I did with Beaupré's nephew, Ovila Lesperance, to try to convince the giant's custodians to relinquish their prize exhibit.

Was it your father or your mother who was related to the giant, Mr. Lesperance?

My mother was a sister of the giant.

Is that what they called him, "the giant"?

At the time, yeah, because he was such an attraction to everybody. You know what it is when something is different. People like to see it and hear about it.

Why did he go away with the circus?

My grandfather wasn't too rich, you know. He thought he could go there and make quite a bit of money.

What was the problem with keeping him at home?

The clothing was the worst problem. At first, he used to wear my grandfather's clothes, until he was around sixteen years old and was too big. But as soon as he got on the tours it never cost him too much for clothing, because all the tailors were glad to make the clothes for the advertisement. In fact, I've got a few suits at home that came from his sister, my aunt.

So the family got the clothes back, eventually. They just didn't get the body.

That's right. At that time out there in Willowbunch, there was no telephone or radio or TV, so when he died in St. Louis the circus didn't want to bother paying his way back to Willowbunch. They told my grandfather he'd be buried there. And that's all he ever heard about it until almost fifteen years later, when he heard that Montreal had bought his body for twenty-five dollars.

What do you want to do with the body?

I don't know. I think he should be buried, especially considering the way they have it there. They have it all naked, you know. Some of my brothers and sisters saw him and they say it's awful to see. Of course, it's in a glass vault, as they call it, but the body should be buried. I think it's funny that the university never tried to get in contact with Willowbunch. I know my grandparents would have sure liked to see his body brought back here if they had known he was there. In 1970 for the Centennial of Willowbunch we made a replica of him from the pictures I had. That's the only thing we've got up here, but he was just like one of the family, you know. He was a giant and that was all.

That plea to give Edward Beaupré a decent burial is still to be fulfilled. Lesperance has been rebuffed by the doctors in Montreal, and the giant continues on in open view − in death, as he had been in life, a monster to be marvelled at. And that's *not* funny.

A chapter about funny people shouldn't end on a down note. To restore the mood, I offer a final funny man, this time a politician, making the ultimate political speech.

This pearl of political oratory was almost lost to history. It was recorded by a CBC newsman at a nominating convention before the 1974 Ontario provincial election, but never played on the news because its special qualities could not be handled within the traditional news format. So Ken McCreath, the reporter who'd gone out to cover the event, brought the tape to *As It Happens*, where we aired it. We felt that it belonged to all Canadians, not just the lucky few who happened to attend the local meeting.

May I suggest that you read the speech aloud in order to apppreciate its charm. The tone you want on this is cheerful bombast. I'm afraid that some opening phrases are missing. It took the reporter a moment or two to collect his wits and start recording.

Our anonymous MPP, by the way, was returned to office at the next Ontario election. The Miss Morrison whom he was there to introduce has not been heard of since. I wonder if she's still even a Tory — imagine having to follow this remarkable address.

> Either we have a thing we believe in or we don't. And if they don't, then get them out. But I happen to believe in those kind of people who believe in the kind of people you are. And I kind of believe that this is the place that I can make the kind of speech that I want to. And if you don't want to make that speech, well, that's fine and dandy.
>
> Oh, you can talk about it. Oh, yes sir, you can talk about *it*. We can talk about it from over here and we can talk about it from over there. And we can talk about it from here and we can talk — but don't you come back to me, or to the people that succeed me a hundred years from now, and say you didn't believe it. Because we're going to come back and we're going to say we rammed it down your throat. And that's the way it's going to be.
>
> [*A gentle nudge here from the Chairman to get on with Miss Morrison's nomination.*]
>
> Yes. And I know we only have four minutes and I'm going to say something. Because, deep down, you know

what we are talking about and beyond that you know what we're *really* talking about. And, you see, we're running out of time. And we're running out of this and we're running out of that.

I'm going to say to you something. That about a year from now you're going to talk about Miss Morrison and about the things she said. But the one thing that I would like you to remember is that regardless of what is said about Miss Morrison, or about this or about that, is that it really fundamentally comes down to the right time to sing. And therefore I am turning over to you, Miss Morrison.

Thank you.

Nine
Building a Better Mousetrap

The inventors I've picked for this chapter are not special for
the impact they've had or for the fortunes they've made.
They're here in recognition of their bull's-eye intuition —
that bang-on ability to define and service the particular
needs of our peculiar times. Each has built a better mousetrap, and if posterity isn't kind to them, at least *As It
Happens* once beat a path to their door.

Armand Henault did not develop "living pottery" to
make himself rich or famous. It just seemed to evolve naturally out of his conviction that funerals were not the better
way. Because he'd never craved attention, it was a lively and
still modest inventor I found on the line, innocent of the
implications of his breakthrough.

How did you get started, Mr. Henault?
    I was talking with a friend of mine in Vermont and I
    decided that, instead of these barbaric funerals, I'd like
    to be made into something. Think of it this way: we use

bone ash now in our pottery and glazes — animal ash from slaughterhouses, ground up fine. Human bone ash is the same thing, so why not use it for pottery. The only difference is that we get the human element mixed in here.

What sort of things do you make out of people's ashes?

I do any kind of vessel that they suggest. They might ask for something that will hold a certain type of flower — orchids or geraniums, or what have you. Some people like to be made into the form of an animal. I have one particular person who I made into a hanging aquarium and there are fish in it. That's putting a little life back into the person. The person loved fish, so I fashioned this hanging planter. There's no end to the things that people want to be made into.

You don't make any kind of judgment on their choice?

Oh, no. Anything that you want.

No request you wouldn't honour?

I can't think of any. I had one woman, if you don't mind my telling you, who sent me her husband's ashes and told me to flush them down the toilet. So I even did that for her. I don't know if she was a nut or what, but I got the ashes and I did that very thing with them.

You're a most amenable gentleman. How much did you charge her for that service?

Well, I told her the basic price for a pot was twenty-five dollars. That's what I get in a gift store for my regular pottery. I don't take advantage of the fact that someone has died. So she sent me the twenty-five dollars. That was making money pretty easy. All I had to do was just pull the latch.

Mr. Henault, do your neighbours know about your activities?

They don't really know because they don't believe it. You know, a philosopher in his own country is without honour. Anyway, I'd rather that they wouldn't know because I don't need busybodies.

In the old days people used to put these ashes in an urn on the fireplace, we're told. So I guess this is no sillier.

Sure, they put them in an urn. That's a little bit morbid,

to look in there and see that. But if you look at the urn itself, and *that* is the person, then you're looking at a work of art that lasts forever. It gets more valuable as time goes on. These pots will be quite valuable. I have a platter, for instance, eighteen inches in diameter, that is used for *hors d'oeuvres* for guests. It's glazed with human bone ash and it looks mosaic and is very beautiful.

How old are you, Mr. Henault?

Sixty-nine.

Maybe you get more philosophical when you're sixty-nine.

Perhaps so, but I haven't had any real cranks yet who object to this, no religious organization or anything. Oh, the morticians give me a little flak once in a while, but all I know is that I would rather be in my garden somewhere, passed around from auction sale to auction sale, than end up in some high-rise mausoleum.

What are you going to be, Mr. Henault?

I want to be a tomcat. I want to be a terracotta tomcat sitting in my garden in Vermont, looking serenely out at the Green Mountains. That's what I prefer to be. But unglazed. Myself, I don't like glazes.

The *entrepreneur* I respond to is the one who exploits the obvious. He sees what's there for everyone to see, but with his special eye he isolates the opportunity that we all missed. Ace Reid, a cowboy in Kerrville, Texas, is such a man. Resentment led him to his big idea.

Tell us about these hats you've got for sale, Mr. Reid.

It dawned on me that the hippies were the ones buying these faded Levis and shirts. They're buying western hats and taking them outside and dropping 'em on the ground, slapping 'em, and knocking them against buildings — anything to make 'em look old and beat-up. And that just makes me real mad, because I'm a cowboy. I was raised during the Depression days in north Texas and we dreamed of having some fresh-looking pants that cost three dollars. Yet these hippies pay forty dollars for their faded-looking pants that have patches on 'em.

Something's screwy.

So I thought I'd just come out with a hat that will suit these kids, because all cowboys sweat their hats out, but a hippie ain't gonna sweat.
What do you make your imitation sweat out of?
I can't tell you that because then our competitors would know what to do.
Well, is it chemical?
It ain't natural sweat, 'course not. That takes ten years, to get natural sweat. This is an artificial sweat and the hippies are thrilled to death. Now they're asking for T-shirts with sweat under the arms.
You're kidding us now.
It's the damndest thing that you ever heard of, Barbara. We got us a winner.
Everyone wants instant experience nowadays.
Instant experience and instant success and instant sweat. You've heard it all here from an old cowboy down in Texas.
Where do you go from here, Ace?
Where do we go from here? They are talking to us now about artificial cow manure to put on boots, and we are working on it. I don't know if we're going to come up with a cow manure smell or not, but we're going to try.

There's no place like California to stimulate the creative juices. In scanning the Los Angeles *Free Press*, the underground weekly whose want ads function as a sort of shopping centre for S and M paraphernalia, swingers' circles, and other west-coast whimsies, two of our industrious story producers happened upon a small boxed ad offering a Howard-Johnson panoply of five fruit-flavoured enemas. This had to be for us.

But how to get such ribaldry past the ridicule of their virtuous colleagues at the daily story conference? Being inventive themselves, they didn't bother. They simply went ahead and dialled. Good sense, of course, prevailed. The interview was recorded but never broadcast, condemned to internal circulation only. Enema-expurgated, I now share

that interview with you. The speaker's name is Bob. He said
he didn't have a second name.

Is this the House of Dominance?
    Yes.
I'm calling from Canada. For the Canadian Broadcasting
Corporation.
    Yes, ma'am.
We'd like to know more about the House of Dominance.
    We'll have to confirm it, ma'am. What is your number
    and we'll call you right back. What part of Canada is it?
It's Toronto.
    Okay. Do me one favour. Then we won't have to call you
    back. Please pronounce a-b-o-u-t.
About. About.
    All right. We'll accept what you're saying. Go ahead.
    What is it you'd like to know about us?
Who do you fear is calling?
    I beg your pardon?
I don't understand who you're afraid is calling.
    We get a lot of peculiar calls.
I'll betcha, with services like yours.
    Okay, how can we help you?
Well, first of all, what does your place look like? When a
client comes in for an appointment, what do you offer him?
    All right. When he comes in, he's met in the reception
    room and offered a printed list with about fifteen differ-
    ent domination items that we do. Then, if he decides on
    one, he's taken either to one of our special rooms or into
    a dungeon. Now, our dungeon is completely equipped,
    with eight exotic pieces of equipment worth well over
    three to five thousand dollars –
Now, just a minute. What are we talking about here? Eight
different ways of tying him to the wall?
    Right. There's the table, a hoist, a spanking stool, a St.
    George's cross, a regular cross, an upside-down cross,
    and an H – what does that make? And a bondage board.
Do you have costumes if he wants?
    It's optional. But basically it's done nude.
And it's dark?

It's done in red light, actually. The dungeon is lit in red.
You hired a decorator, did you, to give you the authentic dungeon feeling?

Oh, no, we designed and built this ourselves.
But it's a modern dungeon? You're not trying to do the sixteenth century again or anything?

Far from it. In fact, it's even air-conditioned.
After you've got him strung up, what do you do to him?

You spank him, you tickle him, you pour wax on him — whatever his trip is. It depends.
It sounds expensive.

It costs thirty dollars for a half hour, or fifty dollars for an hour. That's our basic rate.
It's hard to believe a man could take an hour's worth of that.

Some people could take three hours. We have clients who fly in here from all over the US. And one from Montreal, who just flies here for a two-hour session and flies back. By the way, we operate on an appointment-only basis. There's not fifteen people running around here. It is a discreet location, unmarked.
Something like seeing your psychoanalyst. You don't have to see the next client waiting.

Right.
You offer ladies a first session free. What's your thinking there?

Right. A lot of women are into dominance, but they're very reluctant to go into a professional house of dominance for fear of being exposed, exploited, and God knows what else. And so, in order to ease their apprehension, we offer the first session free.
So she's met at the front door —

You bet. She's put at ease. She is told exactly what will happen and what won't happen to her. And then she is brought into a dungeon and she is dominated — either by a male or a female, depending on her choice.
What do you think of your clients?

I would say this to you, and it may come as some surprise: we have the fringe element and the nuts okay, but they are a very minor group. The people that we do are attorneys, engineers, lawyers, doctors, professional people. I think that we perform a service and if a person wants to use it, fine.

And you're laughing all the way to the bank?

Right.

Oh, my, you're fading. I can hardly hear you, all of a sudden.

What happened?

I don't know. Maybe God doesn't like this item.

Dr. George King, British spiritualist, founder of the International Aetherius Society, communicator with the planet Venus, is also an inventor. Realizing that what the world has always needed is a gizmo that can store the power of personal prayer for concentrated bombardment later, he produced it – a twenty-first-century concept.

How does prayer power work?

Very briefly, I have devised an apparatus which will collect the energy produced by prayer. I can discharge this energy from the prayer-power battery for the benefit of suffering parts of the world. The beauty of the whole thing is this: this battery needs, shall we say, 500 to 600 hours to charge, but its power can be released in something like forty-five minutes. So this is a tremendous concentration.

Dr. King, what's the box made of? How does it accumulate the prayers?

I will only say this about the battery. I think "box" is kind of undertalking the thing a lot. It has a certain type of crystal in it – certain types of picked metals – one of which happens to be gold, not because it's a precious metal but because it will conduct high-frequency energies.

What are you going to do with this power?

We have already discharged two batteries in Operation Prayer Power. The first was discharged on August 20, 1973, to the victims of the Pakistan flood, and the second battery was discharged later in 1973 to the same area. This is the kind of, shall we say, terrestrial crisis that we would discharge our batteries to.

In what way has it helped them?

Probably we'll never know. We don't claim that it's brought about any miraculous result and we're not looking for miraculous results at this particular time. We think the time will come when we probably will have miraculous results, but we're all neophytes and we all believe that we have a lot to learn.

How are you going to keep your prayer accumulator out of the hands of sinister forces? I assume it could be used for ill, too?

That's a fantastically good question. It seems as though the questioner has done his homework. You have a point there. Believe me, you really have a point there. None of the apparatus in Operation — thank you very much for this question, by the way —

You're welcome.

— no, none of the equipment in Operation Prayer Power is for sale. Not at all. Under no account would I dream of selling any of it. There's not enough money to buy me, although I think it will be attempted. And I think you know whom I'm talking about. Unfortunately, these things do happen. Rather than letting the whole thing fall into the wrong hands, I would destroy it.

How are you going to protect your box?

Ah, well, would you want me to make that statement to all and sundry now? Come on. I have ways and means of doing this.

Well, Dr. King, I hope you can stay a force for the good.

I will stay a force for the good, that I'll guarantee — absolutely guarantee it. You know, when you do a certain amount of good in this world, although you have certain interfering forces against you, you also have very powerful forces on your side.

Whom do you mean, there?

I think I'd better leave the statement as it is.

Who says that enterprise is dead? Gynecologists in Japan are making a lot of money with their new wedding service — repairing brides for fussy husbands. Robert Whymant, a journalist in Tokyo for the London *Sunday Times*, investigated the operation to create a hymen.

Is it a complicated operation, Mr. Whymant?

> The operation takes a very, very short time — about seven or eight minutes in all — preceded by about one hour's examination and followed by a couple of hours for the anaesthetic to wear off.

Is it plastic surgery?

> Not really, but it does recreate the hymen artificially with sheep gut, which melts after a month. So the operation has to take place less than a month before the wedding. Some girls come back again and again. These are geisha girls who are sold and who have to be absolutely perfect to be sold at a high price to the new master.

Do they go in secrecy to these doctors?

> Absolutely. The thing has to be done in secret because it's intended as a grand deception for the bridegroom, who sometimes even has detectives trailing the girl. Japanese men still attach a great deal of value to a virgin bride.

I suppose the girls want to hide their condition from their parents, as well.

> No, the astonishing thing is that most of the girls go along with their mothers. It's the mothers who take the girls to these clinics. Nobody knows better than the mother the value of going into marriage untainted by past indiscretions. When they arrive at the clinic, the mother explains the circumstances and then she starts to sob over such dishonourable behaviour, shameful for a well-educated daughter. The doctors listen and pretend they're hearing it for the first time. One girl who had the operation told me that she did it for the sake of her pride. Even though she herself had pretty advanced ideas on sex, she said she wanted to feel clean on that day. She was bending to the chauvinism of men, who still insist on this purity. A survey made by a television program found that 80 per cent of Japanese men still insist on a virgin bride.

While the big boys are inventing World War Three, there's still room for the small *entrepreneur* who is prepared to service the coup-and-revolution business. A best seller at the moment is the Panther BMRV, a bullet- and mine-resistant limousine, with optional extras like a rear-mounted submachine gun, TV, and bar. Bob Jankel, Managing Director of Panther West Winds Sportscar of Byfleet, England, reviewed the features for us. I asked him why he thought the Panther belonged in every dictator's future, rather than a Ford.

Mr. Jankel, how much security are you offering? What can your car withstand?

The idea of this vehicle is to give people who use it a very high degree of protection that one is not able to get in a modern, so-called bullet-proof, limousine. I can't go into ballistics figures, but in broad terms, a modern assassin, using something like an armalite rifle, would be able to penetrate the majority of bullet-proof limousines. This car would withstand that. This vehicle would also withstand a point-five-calibre machine, which is a very, very heavy machine gun; also anti-vehicle mines. This car is completely armoured underneath. It's fitted with bullet-proof tires. Even if the tires were caught in a blast from a land mine, it would just take a section off, but the vehicle would still be mobile.

What's inside those tires?

I can't tell you. That's classified.

How high-powered a motor has it got to drive around that much tin?

It's a seven-litre Chrysler engine that we're using in the vehicle. With automatic transmission and four-wheel drive, the vehicle weighs about nine tons. It's a very modern-looking machine. There's a driver in front who has a guard beside him. And there is a central module, which is completely cut off from both the driver and guard at the front, as well as the two guards who ride in the rear of the vehicle. The centre module can carry up to eight people and is completely air-conditioned and self-contained. It has its own power source. This particular model also has a radio system whereby the owner is in direct contact with his chiefs of staff.

Mr. Jankel, how much of the road is this car going to take up? It sounds huge.

It is a very large vehicle. It is about eight feet wide and about twenty-seven feet long. The module in the centre section is seven feet square. It's almost like a small room, with large glass windows down each side and a closed-circuit television system. By pressing a button, they can see either forwards or rearwards on the screen or pick up a local station if that's required. This model also has a rear-mounted point-five-calibre machine gun.

Is your client planning a coup or trying to withstand one?

I don't know. But the majority of interest that there has been in Europe is from a company that specializes in protecting the senior executives of multinational companies, particularly in Italy, from kidnapping. This vehicle, once it's all closed in and the hatches are tied down, is very nearly indestructible. If somebody used an antitank weapon they'd get in, but very few kidnappers or assassins are using that sort of equipment for the moment.

How much does this little beauty cost?

It depends on the specifications. This particular one has got a lot of deluxe equipment, like bars and mink on the floor and things like that, so this particular one will come out just under $180,000.

What kind of production are you anticipating for this car?

Originally, we thought we would probably make about three or four a year, but the way the enquiries are going, it looks extremely likely that we will be building about one every two weeks. It's unbelievable. Our phone has been going absolutely crazy. It's quite overwhelming, in fact. There is nothing like this in the world, I suppose, and it appears that there's a very, very large demand for it.

Well, it's an unsafe world, Mr. Jankel, but I guess you know that.

A. J. Weberman has always been a good giggle. He's a media regular because he knows how to play with people's outrage. His mousetrap is not a product but a whole new area of human enquiry. He calls it "garbology." Weberman's early digs into the garbagecans in front of the houses of pop stars like Dylan and Nixon were so celebrated that he became a star of the sixties in his own right – worse, Weberman was imitated.

I was once at a story conference at a Canadian magazine where a foray into Canadian celebrity garbage was being blocked out. I was appalled. I mean, some freedoms shouldn't have to be defended. This is surely not a complicated question, like who owns a woman's body. I own my own garbage – right into the truck. Anyway, Weberman defied that logic and made a fortune doing it – in terms of publicity, at least. Alas, it turns out that while Weberman was inventing garbology on his mountaintop, the CIA had long been into it on theirs; although, for obvious reasons, they were unable to copyright their claim.

Mr. Weberman, I read in the British press that the Russian navy is running around the North Sea trying to pick up garbage from NATO warships. And, of course, the only person I wanted to talk to about that was you.

> I hate competition, you know. But it doesn't matter, because the CIA has totally ruined it for me, anyway. Like the embassies in Washington, DC – they're now so garbanoid that they throw nothing away. And the Pentagon has got so uptight that they've removed all the unclassified garbage cans and ordered that everything – toilet paper, everything – be treated as top-secret. I'll say this for them: the CIA is fully aware of the tremendous potential latent in garbified matter. In the early fifties in Vienna, one of their agents slipped an airport garbage concessionaire a thousand dollars for some trash he'd collected from a Russian airliner. If Congress had ever found out that the CIA was spending a thousand dollars on some torn magazines, paper napkins, an empty bottle, a crust of black Russian bread, and a bent coat hanger, it would have led to a Watergate-type scandal twenty years earlier.

What were they looking for, do you think?

What were they looking for! They were looking for anything that would give them information about Russian
air power.

How can a coat hanger help?

Because it's made of shavings from the wings of new
long-range Soviet bombers. Just from the hanger's com-
position you can calculate the range and bomb load of
the plane. So, thanks to garbage, Mr. and Mrs. America
can breathe safely again.

And that's not the only time the CIA was involved in garbage
research.

No. I hate to say it, but the CIA does get the garbology
Beyond-the-Call-of-Duty Award. Part of their clandestine intelligence program includes secretly collecting
samples of foreign leaders' urine and feces.

How did they do that do you think?

I'm not sure of the mechanics involved because, unlike
the CIA, I draw the line.

Do you think the CIA monitors American leaders? How
about Nelson Rockefeller's garbage, for example?

I don't know about Nelson's, but David Rockefeller once
called the Red Squad on me when I went up to his
garbage. Like, I was just checking the garbage out, and
all of a sudden these two guys who had the house under
surveillance jumped out of the car, ran over to me, and
lifted me off the ground and started screaming. "All
right. What in the hell are you putting in that garbage
can?" They thought I was going to put a bomb in there.

But you were taking out?

Right. I said, "I ain't putting it in, I'm taking it out, you
know." They wanted to know if I was crazy.

Does it bother you to learn you've been behind in garbage
research all along?

Fair and square, you know, that's the way it is in garbology. First come, first served.

And finally, Dennis Burkitt who did not *invent* fibre. His
breakthrough was the discovery of its role in human health.
Burkitt preaches fibre, practises fibre, lives fibre. He says

that more bran in your breakfast will prevent gallstones, appendicitis, hemorrhoids, hiatus hernia, and varicose veins, not to mention cancer of the colon. Some people thought Burkitt was a put-on. But I assure you that he is very serious.

Dr. Burkitt, is "food fibre" a fancy name for what our grandmothers used to call "bulk"?

> No. When I talk about fibre it's more a chemical concept. It's the fibre in food that profoundly influences the amount of stool you pass daily.

More stools being good?

> More stools being good. Small hard stools being bad; large soft stools being good.

And you can have the right kind of stool if you eat the right amount of fibre?

> Right. We have never found a community that passed large soft stools that got anything other than a low prevalence of the common diseases filling Canadian hospitals today, such as pulmonary heart disease – the commonest cause of death; gallstones – the commonest abdominal operation; appendicitis – the commonest emergency operation; varicose veins, and so on. We have so neglected the size of stools that I still find it difficult in North America to get any information as to the amount of stool the average North American passes per day. People are trying to do this for us now, but it's some of the hardest information to get.

Well, unlike you, Dr. Burkitt, most people still find this a difficult area to deal with.

> When I go to India and Pakistan and similar countries, what I look at is stools. Of course, it's much easier to look at stools in a country with no toilets, because you've only got to get up in the morning, walk along the roadside and the field, bring your camera with you, and you photograph the stools.

You don't!

> I do. And I use these in lectur   I'll be using them in my lecture tomorrow. The local population thinks I'm quite

mad, of course, but this is a blind spot in medicine and it's of tremendous, supreme significance, I believe.

You're talking about very serious diseases, so why am I laughing?

It's very serious. What's happened is that we've taken the good part out of our food and we've given it to the horses and donkeys. We've got fit donkeys and fit horses and sick people. We want to get the donkey food back on the human table.

Ten
Barbara Antagonistes

I used to share a television studio with an interviewer who not only verbally abused his guests, but every once in a while would get so caught up in the discussion that he had to be physically restrained from throttling his startled subjects before they could escape the set. That's not a style of interviewing I've ever liked. Not that I like the straight-out seduction session any better; in that one the interviewer courts his guest – whether man or woman – with appreciative chuckles, a few flattering questions, perhaps a self-deprecating remark or two, and then – having successfully charmed his quarry – and only then, does this seductive type decide what he wants from his fascinated guest. It's a useful approach – practised, for some reason, more by men than women – but one I've never been comfortable with, either.

It's not that I don't like to be liked. But being liked has never struck me as a pre-condition for an effective interview. When your guests aren't obliged to like you, or you them, you can't beat the liberty and possibility that opens up on all sides. I would like to think that most of the interviews I do are conducted in an atmosphere of cordiality and even warmth. But every once in a while something in the voice – something in the sound of an answer – gets to me. The adrenalin surges, and before I realize it I'm going for broke: what makes him think he can get that one by me?

There was a psychiatrist in London, Ontario, for example, who'd managed to get himself some press attention by attaching a pitch for psychiatric half-way houses to the eye-catching claim that large mental hospitals were themselves driving people crazy. His half-way house proposal sounded worthy enough; but what was this, I asked, about hospitals creating madness? Would you give us an example of that?

"No," he replied, "I won't."

Hmn, I thought, suddenly curious. "Why not?"

"Because I don't want to," he spit back.

This guy had to be kidding. "Why won't you?"

"Because I won't."

That's all it takes, I'm ashamed to say, to turn me into a terrier. I wouldn't relent. This was his idea, after all about hospitals creating craziness instead of curing it, not mine. What did he mean he didn't want to discuss it? Just as stubbornly, the doctor refused to offer a single instance to back up his claim. Our scrapping, of course, completely distracted him from his pitch for government funding for his pet project. Serves him right, I've always figured. Maybe next time he won't make claims that he's not prepared to prove.

I rarely indulge myself in that kind of testiness. I don't remember ever beginning an interview with the intent to injure. Occasionally I'll come on tough, or order a guest to remove her impenetrable sunglasses, ·as I once did to a woman who'd planned to spend the interview sheltered behind her shielding lenses. But when I do that, it's not to start ahead, but to start even.

The exchanges in this chapter started out as straightforward interviews but ended as collisions. If you measure them by the amount of information extracted, they're all failures. For excitement, however, they're tops.

The most adrenalinized high of all for me has to be my

radio meeting with Sandra Good. The moment the wires flashed the news that Lynette "Squeaky" Fromme (pronounced as in "home," please, not "hum") had tried to shoot US President Ford in front of the California State Legislature in Sacramento, we were on the phone dialling for her roommate and fellow Manson family member, Sandra Good.

We knew that Fromme and Good were a team, because our show had picked up on them just a couple of months before, when these two burned-out young women released to the press a garbled piece of threatening prose, which somehow linked pollution with political treachery: "If Nixon's face [meaning Ford] continues in office, it will be bloodier than the Tate-La Bianca murders and My Lai combined." At the time, that message struck us as little more than the last venomous ravings of the satanic Manson gang, and we'd presented Good's ramblings that night almost as a brightener — a see-what-they've-come-to sort of piece. Three months later, Fromme's attempt on Ford's life proved us very wrong.

We found Good easily. She was revelling in yet another round of press attention and holding forth from the apartment that the Manson girls had shared until four days before, when Fromme went downtown to gun down Gerald Ford. Good was feeling bloody-minded, that was clear. From the moment she came on the line — even from the belligerent way she said "Hello" — her attitude was pugnacious and disdainful. The question was: how many minutes did I have before she punished me by hanging up?

There was an unnerving lunacy about the interview. I was pushing against this unspoken deadline, desperately trying to find out about her roommate. But all she would tell me about was the need for saving the fish and the trees. She had the friends who carved up people as casually as Sanders carves up chickens; but I was the one who was put down for my appetite for sensationalism.

The interview incensed a lot of listeners and puzzled many others. Was she crazy or was she evil? Part of her message sounded almost reasonable. Even now, after all these months, I'm occasionally asked how I managed to stay so calm despite the spew of venom directed at me. Actually, I'm not convinced that I handled that interview at all well. Once I realized that Good was prepared to give me only a speech, I had a dilemma. She was never going to tell me anything insightful about Fromme. So what to do? Sit there and accept it? Or take a chance on provoking her? I chose the second, hoping for a glimpse of the mad space that Fromme and Good were in.

Miss Good, have you had any contact with Lynette Fromme since her arrest?
　No.
Have you been able to see her?
　No.
Have you been able to communicate with her?
　No.
Can you tell us the condition you last saw her in? When did you see her last?
　　We had been looking at the state of this country and of the world and it's a mess. It's a big mess and it needs cleaning up. If people are going to survive, change is necessary. There are many, many people, thousands of people, children included, who are tired of the destruction of the environment, the wildlife, rivers, the oceans, cutting down of trees, and —
Miss Good, could we talk about that in a minute?
　　Yeah.
Could you tell us more about Lynette Fromme first?
　　I'm answering your question.
No, I asked you when was the last time you saw Lynette Fromme.
　　Listen, these picayuney questions really don't mean — I don't understand what you're getting at. This is a reflection — rather than looking at the little picayuney details of when she got up or her particular state of mind — it's irrelevant. There are a lot of roots to problems that people have, a world people, a nation people. There are certain acts that reflect problems.
What do you think about what happened in Sacramento?
　　That also is a rather ignorant question. What do I think

about it? I think it's time that this country started taking a look at itself, taking a look at its problems, and not hold positive solutions to the problems down.

All right. Miss Good, if you wouldn't mind, let's hear a little bit more, please, about when you last saw Lynette Fromme and what kind of shape she was in.

That question shows your ignorance and I won't answer it.

How about this, then? Can you tell us anything about Harold Boro, the man who gave that gun to Lynette?

No. That question also shows your ignorance of the greater problems that are going to jump down your throat if you don't take a look at them.

Do you know Harold Boro?

I'm saying that the people better start taking a look at the problems, not the picayuney incidents. I'm saying, look at the roots of these problems. Many people all over the world are due to be assassinated. This is just the beginning of many, many assassinations that are going to take place.

Miss Good, how come you're talking about trees that you care about and yet you don't mind killing men?

Men that kill life, that kill harp seals, that kill trees, that poison oceans and rivers and air are killing all of us because we need these things to live. Start looking at your world, woman. Start looking at the world you're leaving for your kids and quit putting sensational news stories and what you look like and your social position over life.

Miss Good, do you think any —

Listen, woman —

Pardon?

Don't probe me like that. You listen to what I'm saying and you tone your manner of questioning down or I'll hang up. Do you understand me?

Well, I'm prepared for your hanging up. You know, that's one of the risks.

You're prepared for what you want to hear. You're not going to get what you want to hear. Listen, put me onto somebody else. I don't like you.

Why not?

    Trouble. Because you're probing me with what's in your mind and I'm trying to tell you things as I see them, not as you wish me to tell you, not as a —

Tell us about Charles Manson then.

    Let's start this all over again.

Okay. Tell us about Charles Manson.

    You go to him yourself.

You have been quoted as saying that his job is to straighten out the world.

    His job? It's your job, woman. It's your job. He's been left out of this world's madness. You'd better pray he'll help you fix yourselves up. You'd better pray. It's your job, woman, to start making gardens rather than pushing your husbands to destroy things. Start talking to the executives, the killers of wildlife and of the Earth. You stop. There's a wave of assassins called the International People's Court of Retribution and they're watching you.

Was the attack on President Ford justified, then?

    Yes. Any attack on any life is justified. Any attack on anyone who puts money and lies over people's lives is justified. There'll be many, many killings, many killings. Best you be willing to open your mind and look at the roots of problems. Look at the problems that are besetting your world, your country.

Miss Good, let's talk about killing for a minute, okay? You say —

    Listen, woman, put me onto somebody else. I can't talk to you.

Why?

    You're a very, very bad reporter. You're very bad. Put me onto somebody else. You're one of the worst, really. You really are. You're very rude, very imperceptive, you're very ignorant. Your technique is just crude. You don't have any finesse. Now put me onto somebody else.

I'm it, Miss Good. I'm it, I'm afraid.

    Are you a man or a woman?

I'm a man.

    Are you a man? You are a woman.

Well then, why did you ask?

> Because you reflect a woman's fear. Your unwillingness
> to look at problems.

I see. And you?

> I reflect a lot of children. I reflect a lot of people with
> concern for the Earth and the children —

Miss Good, children grow up to be men and women.

> All right, in your sense. In the robot, computerized,
> slave-for-the-dollar sense, go-to-school-and-spend-
> your-life-in-a-book sense, or living-life sense. What are
> you talking about?

You say you talk for children, yet you talk of killing men.

> I'm talking about people who will be killed. Don't inter-
> rupt me again. When I talk about killing I'm saying that
> there will be a wave of assassins killing those who are
> killing the environment, the wildlife, the trees, selling
> products to the children, and the people —

Miss Good?

> Don't interrupt me.

Miss Good?

[Click. She was gone.]

In November of 1973 *As It Happens* did not go to the
Soviet Union. That's remarkable, considering how much
everybody wanted us to go. The CBC was enthusiastic—bouncing five days of live programming off Anik from
Moscow to Canada would be a pretty neat way to show off
the capacities of the brand-new satellite. The Department of
External Affairs was gung-ho, because it thought a little bit
of Canadian show-biz would help along *détente*. Certainly
the State Radio Committee in Moscow was keen. What an
opportunity to show a coast-to-coast Canadian audience the
new and friendly face of Soviet socialism. We saw it as an
adventure, a chance to break new ground. We would be the
first to broadcast serious opinion and information live from
the communist world – something nobody had ever done.

In all the excitement of getting Russian visas, Russian
phrase books, and Russian background, I was the hesitant
one, the one who saw pitfalls when everyone else seemed to
see only glory. A week of Bolshoi ballerinas, gymnasts,

cosmonauts, and electrical engineers would be great, but would we also be able to talk about Soviet Jews, psychiatric man-handling of dissidents, and political meddling in the Middle East? What I was afraid of was that we'd get all the way to the Soviet Union only to end up being – and sounding – used.

Given my cynical turn of mind, I couldn't see why the Russians would have it any other way. The negotiated compromise was this: if we would work from a list of fifty topics acceptable to their Radio Committee, the Soviets would live with a difficult two or three. On the basis of that, our Executive Producer, Mark Starowicz, took off for Moscow to arrange the final details.

In Moscow, however, he discovered that the Soviets understood the deal to contain an extra couple of points. In their version, the Russians would not only be determining *who* would be heard on air on the agreed-to fifty subjects, but they also wanted a typewritten list of all our questions in advance. If it wasn't for the fact that the demand was so insulting, it would have been really funny. Not only did Starowicz not know what directions my interviews would take, I'm often surprised myself. And so, after almost a year of trying to finesse the foxy Soviets, Mark came home and we unpacked our bags.

While all our wheeling and dealing was going on, the President of the American Psychiatric Association, Dr. Alfred Freedman, did go to Moscow to see for himself how psychiatric patients in the Soviet Union are treated, and to check out charges of abuse. From reading reports of his trip, it was obvious that Freedman had been politely sidetracked by the Soviets. Yet, when he came on the air with me, he acted as though his trip had been a breakthrough. I was startled. I'd have thought, considering how neatly he and his team had been checkmated, that a logical response would have been annoyance or embarrassment.

I remember being put off by the way Freedman kept ducking the issue. I couldn't understand why a highly-trained, well-briefed observer, who'd been given a chance to visit the infamous Serbsky Institute and to question some of its more controversial "patients," didn't have at least a couple of stories to tell about what he'd seen there. Why, for goodness sake, had he bothered going – if not to check out accusations that political dissenters, in the name of therapy, are given punishing sulphur injections, are reduced to torpor with chemical depressants, and are even beaten to death by their "nurses"? Even the Communist parties of France and Italy are gagging on the abuse of Soviet psychiatry to deny human rights. How could this eminent American practitioner come away seeming so unperturbed?

I've included all of our early exchanges, with Freedman's carefully worded, defensive responses, in order to justify – perhaps to myself as much as to you – the collision that followed.

Dr. Freedman, my recollection is – correct me if I'm wrong – that on this trip that you've just returned from, one of the motives was to remedy a failure on the part of American psychiatrists to get involved in the issue of uses and abuses of psychiatry within the Soviet Union.

There had been, as you know, allegations concerning the use of psychiatric facilities for the involuntary detention of political dissenters over the last several years. As president of the American Psychiatric Association, I sent a cablegram to the president of the Soviet society, indicating our concern in regard to the allegations.

Were you able to check anything out?

Unequivocally, no. We could not review in detail and examine cases in the manner I would have preferred. I think that we are left still rather questioning. I think I'm much better informed now than I was before, but I don't think we are able to give an unequivocal answer now.

Did you have an opportunity to meet any people described as dissidents?

The only occasion that did arise was at the start of our meeting at Serbsky. It was announced that General Grigorenko, who is one of the well-known cases, would be available for interview. They suggested that two Western psychiatrists accompany two Soviet psychiatrists, one of whom spoke English, to interview General Grigorenko. Well, when they got there, General Grigorenko refused to talk to them. He said he would only speak in the presence of his own interpreter, who was his wife.

Was that denied him?

Well, she wasn't there.

How up-tight about this subject did you find the Soviet equivalents to yourself?

They were upset, I'd say, by the continuing allegations from the West. And they were particularly disturbed by statements that appeared to question the integrity and morality of Soviet psychiatrists — their lack of professionalism. I think that the British medical journal in an editorial, for example, had referred to Soviet psychiatrists prostituting themselves. This they found insulting and very disturbing. As one said to me, "You are rather too responsive to — almost controlled by — your mass media. It's the mass media that's raising all these issues." I pointed out that there is serious concern in the West for humanitarian reasons, as well as our desire not to see our field of psychiatry besmirched in any way.

But you didn't feel able to press it any further than that?

Members of our board who were interested wrote to Soviet psychiatrists. I think this in a sense was a breakthrough; they were saying, "We'll answer any question that you have."

But, from what you've been telling us, it was no breakthrough at all. You didn't get to see anything. You didn't get to learn anything. And you didn't get to press any points to your satisfaction.

Well, I wish you well on your trip to the Soviet Union. I suggest that you go and insist upon meeting privately dissidents whose names you may have. I wish you the best of luck. I am merely telling you that in the course of negotiations and discussions over several years, this is the first time that a group of Soviet psychiatrists have been willing to sit down with an equivalent group and even discuss the issues. If you are unimpressed, then I have no more to say.

But are you satisfied? I guess that's the point I'm getting at.

I'm not satisfied. I think that it's naive of you to raise the question. I mean, you're poorly informed.

Well, I'm certainly always prepared to be naive. I'm just surprised that you think it's a breakthrough. I think that's maybe naive.

I think you're not familiar with the history of the issues. You know, Prometheus getting fire may not seem much of a breakthrough to us, at the present day, but it made a difference. It's a foolish discussion, I must say. So if it's trivial and not interesting to you then we can skip it.

Please, Dr. Freedman, it's hardly trivial or we wouldn't have called you and it's hardly trivial or you wouldn't have gone.

Right. And it was a very draining experience. So if you're interested in it and think it important, then we can discuss it. But if you consider it all a waste of time, then I have something else I'd rather do.

I hardly consider it a waste of time. I just would like to know a bit more about how the issue was handled by the Soviet psychiatrists. If there was any explanation offered at all, if you thought they were caught in a double bind, perhaps, wanting to seem honourable practitioners of an honourable profession, but in some way also feeling politically used?

No, on the contrary, the impression I gained was that the system was such that, without impuning their motives or practices, and considering diagnostic categories and concepts of Soviet justice, that one could say that they were practising in accordance with the general notions of the present time for the Soviet Union. We would not have a comparable situation here.

Did any people in your delegation confront their Soviet equivalents with any cases?

Confront them?

Yes.

No. They presented us with many of the most highly publicized cases.

And what explanation did they give?

The explanation for all of them was that, according to their criteria and their diagnosis, these were seriously disturbed individuals who needed hospitalization. The hospitalization was not because of these individuals' criticism, but because they were mentally disturbed.

And did they outline their criteria?

Some of them are fairly well known. The diagnostic criteria for schizophrenia in the Soviet Union is much broader than those we use in the United States and Canada. But they would say to that, "Well, that's your practice, this is our practice. And we are operating under Soviet laws and those are not discussable."

In five years of almost nightly interviews about murder and mayhem in the Middle East, I've tried to be calm, flat, and cool in asking questions about the day's events, even though often I'm in pain and in passionate disagreement with the person on the other end. No matter how many letters go to the president of the CBC suggesting that I'm a Zionist agent with "ingenious techniques" and an "insatiable appetite for propaganda"; no matter how much my phone rings at home because some irate Jewish listener wants to ask me, "What kind of a Jew are you to be sympathetic to the Arabs?", I've got a very clear conscience about my even-handedness on this most difficult of political dilemmas. By "even-handedness" I don't mean the "fairness" of the row-boat style of journalism that's fashionable now: first we pull for one side, now we pull for the other.

I did lose my cool once, however, and that was in a face-to-face interview with PLO spokesman Shafik Al-Hout. Al-Hout was in Toronto as part of the PLO new-look diplomatic offensive, organized to follow up on Arafat's stunning breakthrough at the UN General Assembly. The decision to book him created great tension in our office. My colleagues know I offer no one an easy platform without challenge, and were uneasy for me. Other interviewers at CBC had refused to talk to him. I knew that if I insisted on a description of the new PLO plan for peace instead of another re-hashing of old grievances, I'd get sucked into looking like an advocate for the other side – a prospect which made *me* uneasy for me.

Al-Hout couldn't lose and I'm sure he knew it. He had an additional advantage. On the previous evening, a hooting, jeering crowd of Jews had prevented Al-Hout from addressing a public meeting, making him seem an oppressed underdog to millions of Canadians who revere free speech and objectivity. Given that fortuitous PR victory, my options were suddenly limited. If I pressed him for anything more than the speech he'd come to give, I'd be vulnerable to accusations of suppressing his point of view. Still, I was determined to advance the discussion past rhetoric about peace and justice to a realistic discussion of whether Palestinians and Israelis could ever live together. If the PLO could insist that they were no longer simply a terrorist organization but rather a government in exile, it seemed appropriate to hear about government policy, such as a plan for peace. And if pressing for answers was to be misconstrued as partisanship, well, that was something I'd just have to live with.

Mr. Al-Hout, I would like to talk to you about the future.

> If we can afford to speak about the future without mentioning the present, we would be doing a miracle.

I want to know how you are going to convince the Israelis that this is a time for diplomacy, that this is a time when guns are to be put away.

> As a matter of fact, we have started our attempts to convince the Israelis and the whole world that we are striving for peace based on justice.

Let's hear the shape of that peace.

> The peace? We are hoping to have an everlasting peace. But I think honestly that without having justice maintained for people in the area, and particularly Palestinian people who are suffering now, I can hardly tell how we could ever maintain peace.

Do you have a concrete agenda? Do you have proposals? Can we get past point-making? Can we hear what you are for?

> In the first place we have to come to an agreement about principles to solve the problem of the Palestinian people.

Is there an Israel in your future, for example?

> There are Jews in my future.

Is there a state called Israel in your future?

> That depends on what kind of an Israel you are referring to. If doctrine —

Is there a state called Israel in your future?

If there is a state and a Zionist state, I will be honest enough to tell you that the struggle will continue. Not necessarily armed struggle, but there is going to be ideological struggle, a political struggle, economic and otherwise. This I am sure of because it happens that we adopt contradictory ideologies.

Mr. Al-Hout, Canada does not tell the United States how to run its life. The United States, hopefully, isn't going to tell Canada how to run its life. Do you see an Israel of the Israelis' own choosing in your future? After all, you don't tell Egypt how to live. You don't tell Syria.

That's very true and I think you are right. I would accept an Israeli sovereignty over all the Jewish legal properties they have in Palestine, but not outside that Jewish property. Legal property that is theirs and not somebody else's. On their own land, they are free. They can choose any system they want. I think they are entitled to that right, but not on any territory that doesn't belong to them or that they took by force.

You know and I know and the world knows that the Israelis are never going to move out of Haifa voluntarily and they're never going to move out of Tel Aviv and they're never going to move out of Jaffa and they're never going to move out of Jerusalem. So what are we talking about? What are the realities? Where do we go?

My dear friend, you are referring to a very horrible reality, which has been based on brute force. Force is not an international law and it is not an everlasting law. They had it once by force. If we accept that law, you are implying that I am entitled to the same right, when I have force, to chase them out of Haifa. So we should try to find a ground, to seek a solution, outside the law of force, which is, unfortunately –

That's what I'm asking you. What is the shape of it? What does it look like?

You are asking me about the map of Israel at a time when the Israelis themselves have never defined their own boundaries and their own maps.

Mr. Al-Hout, I would just like to know once in my life what

in fact the Palestinian Liberation Organization is standing for. You constantly make the point that the Israelis won't sit down and talk to you, but we never can hear from you what you want to talk about.

We want to talk about the implementation of Palestinian national rights in their own homeland.

In what shape?

There are so many shapes. There are so many resolutions which have been rejected by the Israelis. Take one, I give you one shape.

No, no, no. Not one shape. What is *the* shape?

It is the repatriation of the Palestinians, their return to their homeland. And then, as normal citizens, with the rest of the population, to make the kind of regime they want. If I am from Jaffa I'll go back to Jaffa with the rest of the people from Jaffa who want to go there. We have the right to participate in the kind of system that we would like to have in our country, with the rest of the Jews who are living there. That might be a way.

States define their own immigration policy. This country does as well. Canada decides who can come in and who cannot —

Sure. But I haven't recognized Israel. I don't accept Israeli policy and I haven't recognized Israel as a state. I am still in a state of war with Israel because I claim that Palestine is my country and it has been taken by force. And, as long as we didn't come to any settlement, I am fighting back.

So then it's still an either/or situation. There is no way that you can see both states co-existing, and the killing will continue.

Not necessarily.

Until it goes your way?

Not necessarily. There are parts of Palestine that even Israel till now has not said "It's part of Israel" — the Gaza strip, the West Bank — although they are trying to Zionize these areas. They are building colonies on land that doesn't belong to them in the Jordan Heights, in Sinai. That means that Israel today is all of Palestine and

177

part of Sinai and part of the Jordan Heights. I tell you frankly, this will never be accepted, neither by the Arabs nor by the Palestinian people.

How can you expect the Israelis to negotiate with people who don't see a future for them?

Well, I think by more strikes they will see. If we strike them more and they feel that they have to find a way, that will motivate their grey cells for a better policy by which we can co-exist. But if, as it stands now, there's no room for us except on the battlefield, as Mr. Rabin has said, then it's not our mistake.

And that includes terrorism?

Fighting, struggling, madame.

With stars you don't do an interview, you do a deal — and, if you ask me, the deal is rarely worth it. You both know the star's only talking to you because he has to hustle his movie, flog his book, or promote his show. Because of that, you also know that he's going to do everything he can to keep the session superficial. When you're on the whirlwind tour ("If this is Toronto and it's 7:15, you must be Barbara Frum"), you can get awfully good at that. The odd time I've tried for more depth in a celebrity encounter, the look of panic and betrayal has quickly driven me back to banalities.

I once asked George C. Scott how he could sneer at the Academy Awards for tackiness and make a big deal out of not showing up to get an Oscar, yet turn up on the Merv Griffin Show as a panelist on the topic of Hollywood divorce. One raised eyebrow later, I was back to lobbing up the easy ones — "So where are you going from here, George?"

That kind of thing has happened to me so many times that you'd wonder how I could have thought I'd get anything significant from the writer Jan Morris, especially when I knew she had more reason than most to protect her privacy. Jan Morris used to be the English writer James Morris, until she was liberated from her unwanted self by hormone therapy and the surgical knives of a Casablanca sex-change clinic. Boy, did I have questions.

This was the spring of 1974, when everybody's favourite

topic was the difference between what is male and what is female. Coming to my studio was the most incredible of creatures – someone who'd been both. In what sense was Jan Morris now a woman? Are men and women the same except for hardware, after all? What about all the conditioning and acculturation that made Morris, when she was James, climb Mount Everest with Hillary, made her sign on as a war correspondent, made her father four children, for God's sake? And why, when all she'd really done was re-jig some plumbing and redistribute her appendages, was she now a demure and fluttery creature for whom the height of flattery was a wolf whistle in the streets? My curiosity was to be confounded.

A pre-interview lunch was arranged so that we could get comfortable with each other. Exactly the opposite happened. I was put off by her and she by me. Let me put my case as generously as I can: I didn't find her convincing. The voice was wrong, the mannerisms were embarrassing, and her joy and sweetness, which should have been touching, instead were cloying. Most of all, I couldn't stop my eyes from wandering to her shaven chin.

On her side, I suspect that my scrutiny frightened and perhaps revolted her. "We are not going to talk about my family," she announced. Also *verboten* was to be any discussion of what was dubbed her "anatomical conformation." In their place Jan Morris offered me "magic" and the sweet mysteries of femininity.

After lunch we taped our interview. It was as crosspurposed as our lunch, full of evasions, dead-ends, and false trails. When I'd finally worn myself out and called it quits, Jan Morris breathed at me: "You aren't comfortable with me, are you?" I had to concede that I was not.

Miss Morris, when was the earliest moment that you reached this conviction that you were a woman in a man's body?
    It's the earliest memory of my life. I was three or four
    years old – very strange.
And you got married still thinking that you would just live your life as a man?

Yes, I think I was, really. I confided in Elizabeth before I was married to her, but I simply didn't know what it was or what one could do about it – if anything could be done about it – or whether I just had to submerge it. I was not the sort of man who looked ambivalent or homosexual or anything like that. I looked very ordinary, really.

When you decided to do something about it, how long did the transformation take?

I suppose eight to ten years, something of that nature, because it's a long, long process of hormone treatment.

What was that period like?

In some ways it was very distressing and tormenting, otherwise it was rather fun.

Because you're neither.

Quite.

You're not yourself and you're not the person you want to be.

And nobody knows what you are and you're not sure, either.

Did you experience ridicule in that period?

Ridicule, no – bewilderment, self-amusement. I was brought up in a society which was amused by itself and I was amused by myself.

Did you look funny to yourself?

Funny odd, not funny hah-hah.

But did it make you embarrassed or ashamed or uncomfortable?

Well, I'm a winner, you know, to be honest with you. I expect to win and – touch wood – I do. So, no. It was up to me what I looked like, wasn't it? If people were surprised by me, it was up to them. The awkward moments were when purely technical issues arose, when it was necessary to be known which I was – like going through the security check at an airport, that sort of thing. That was embarrassing.

I'm quite sure you realize that there is this fascination with you and your story. A lot of people think that it's for prurient reasons. But I think it goes beyond that, because men and women, people who think about these issues, are all struggling at the moment with what's a man and what's a woman, and they see in you this perfect person to tell us finally.

Was that a question?

Yes. Does that kind of thing fascinate you at all?

I'm in a different realm of thought from most people who want to talk about these issues, because in the first place I differentiate profoundly between sex and gender. I believe them to be two totally different things. But beyond that, I believe that femininity — as against femaleness — can be applied to things, not merely to people and to animals, but to attitudes, conceptions, even to inanimate objects. I wouldn't have changed my gender for anything in the world. I was quite happy with that. What I wanted to change was the sex which had been imposed upon that gender. Gender is what you yourself believe yourself to be. It's also things like talent and tone of voice, the spring of your step — all those intangible things that make up the corpus of the personality. This, to me, is infinitely more important than what happens to be the conformation of your body.

I guess that what's so difficult to get at is that you believe that you were female all along, whereas everyone who meets you wants to hear about how a man turns into a woman.

Yes, quite. That is a difference of approach and I'm afraid I can't resolve it.

What happened to your family? What's happened to your marriage?

We were, naturally, divorced — obviously — but we remain profoundest of friends. In fact, we talked to each other on the telephone this very morning. I spend half the time in her house and she spends a good deal of the time in mine.

Has this not been a mind-blowing experience for her?

No, I don't think so.

Forgive me, but anyone who has lived in a more run-of-the-mill marriage is going to listen to you saying that and be absolutely amazed.

I am amazed that they are. So many people have said that this is bewildering. It seems to me that the nature of a love like ours — which I would assume to be the nature of love in most true marriages — is so limitless and so profound and unshakeable that if you simply happen to change the shape of your body, that's one of the lesser

things of life. If she had wanted to change into a horse I
would, within reason, have loved her.

But, if you'll forgive me, she married a different person.

She married a different body, that's what you're saying,
isn't it? She didn't marry a different essential me. She
didn't marry a different soul, if that's not too preten-
tious a word for it. She's known that innermost part of
me ever since we met.

Is it possible that sex was not a huge component in your
marriage, so that for your wife it's no great loss?

You should ask her, really. I can't answer for her, but it
is true. I was — physical sex has never been a terribly
important part of my thinking.

Is that still true?

Yes, certainly yes. But the compensation I've had for
that has been a sort of heart-on-sleeve purple passion, a
sensual, emotional response to all sorts of other things. I
think, for example, when I look out the window at Venice
on a moonlit night, with some claret or burgundy inside
me and with somebody I love beside me and a moon up
there, and with the smell of age and magic and all, I think
it's a truly sexual lust that I'm feeling there, really.

If it hasn't been mind-blowing for your wife, what's it been
like for your children?

You shouldn't really ask me questions about other people's reactions and emotions, because it's unfair to them.
I can only say that all of us have been linked by this
truest kind of love and it remains so. We've all helped
each other through this thing and I don't think our
relationship has greatly changed as a result of it.

How do they address you or consider you?

Oh, they call me Jan and they — oh, I don't know what
they think of me, they just think of me as Jan, I think.
When this first happened, Elizabeth and I had to establish some sort of ostensible relationship. We used to call
each other sisters-in-law, and therefore people used to
assume that I was the children's aunt. But now that it's
all so public they think of me as a person. The whole
thing has a miraculous magical flavour for me. And my
relationship with them has that, too, you know. It's
something inexplicable and actually very beautiful.

Let me tell you about Jan Morris' final revenge on me. Because of her publicity schedule, our interview had been taped at two in the afternoon for broadcast on that evening's program. While the item was going out on the network, some of the crew drifted into the booth to listen with me. Within moments they were joking and talking about how Jan Morris had handled the allegedly formidable Frum, and about the pain she must have endured to turn from male to female. Suddenly the tape was coming to an end. I was signalled from the control room that we were about to go back on the air live. So I turned to my wise-cracking friends and commanded, "Okay, fellas, *cut it off*."

What a mistake, and not my first. It will take in-depth analysis someday to discover why I so often and so unintentionally *double-entendre*. Anyway, there I was with two story producers and Harry Brown, my co-host at that time. The three of them were doubled over, trying to muffle their laughter so that they would not be heard over the now-open mikes. Harry, who sat opposite me, finally had to put his head on the table and cover it with his hands, although his body continued to twitch in full view.

And with our bewildered producer looking on helplessly through the sound-proof control-room glass, unable to grasp how three staffers could have been struck down simultaneously by convulsions, I embarked on a page-long script about supertankers and the growing risks of hijacking on the open seas.

I couldn't do it. I started. I broke up. I restarted, allowed my eye to wander to Harry's twitching body, and approached hysterics. A long silent pause to regain control. I *had* to do it.

I had it now. But a sob of suppressed panic broke in my throat and reduced me to a giggling fool again.

I never did get through that script. My memory is that somebody, somewhere, read the last few sentences – I really can't say who. I just remember the pleasure of finally abandoning myself to laughter, tears of relief coursing down my cheeks. To this day that stretch of tape, with me laughing my head off about blackmail on the high seas, is nailed to the wall of *As It Happens*, a warning reminder to all producers of the fallibility of hosts.

Acknowledgements

One of the nicer things about writing a book is that you get a chance to thank publicly those whom you can never really thank enough. In my case, that means my friends and colleagues – the people behind the scenes at *As It Happens*. It's thanks to them that a million Canadians find it worthwhile to tune in to *As It Happens* at least once a week. It's because of their talent and their generosity and their high spirits that the last five years have been such a joyride for me.

Turning out the program is a pressure-cooker of a job. Everyone who's done a stint with us has been radically – and, I suspect, permanently – changed by the experience. We all seem to end up speaking faster, thinking faster, and even moving faster. You find yourself at first unconsciously, and then quite deliberately, judging everything you hear or read and everyone you meet in terms of their program potential – would this make an item for the show?

Over five years, dozens of people have joined us, some for short runs, some for long, all helping to feed the monster for a while before going on to calmer occupations. For each of them I feel enormous affection and gratitude.

Mark Starowicz was our Executive Producer for the past three years. More than anyone, Mark understood the potential of the format and had the panache and energy to realize the possibilities. While I did the interviews in the studio downstairs, he paced, yelled, motivated, and inspired in the offices upstairs. It was Mark who made *As It Happens* into a news-gathering machine, and it was he who made everyone who worked on staff believe that *As It Happens* was the most exciting journalistic enterprise going. A mix of the most unlikely and contradictory impulses, he is alternately sentimental and cynical, lovable and irascible, ultra-opinionated and yet scrupulous about detail. It was his cross in life that there just weren't enough big stories in the world to exhaust his flair for covering them.

My on-air partner, the aristocratic Alan Maitland, "Lord Maitland Snacks," feeds me all day and makes seven hours together in the studio one unending joy. His first love, I fear, is horses and the sport of kings. It's our good fortune that he's willing to bring his grace, humour, and magic vocal chords downtown every day to give *As It Happens* its zip and authority.

Richard Bronstein we always considered the most gracious and gentle of men. The government of Ian Smith, on the other hand, considered him so formidable that they issued an order expelling him from Rhodesia before he'd even arrived to prepare a special *As It Happens* documentary.

Max Allen is a rug merchant who turns out blockbusting documentaries on the side.

Beverley Reed, Trudie Richards, and Helga Abraham were the super-sleuths no one could escape. Beverley was the most dogged of them all, with one specialty – unlisted numbers. Helga once spent five hours tracking down an OPEC official to a hotel in Tripoli. When a befuddled Mr. Martin was finally roused out of bed and explained, "No, I'm the Martin who's in travel; you want the Martin who's in oil," Helga momentarily lost control and hollered down the line in total frustration, "Are you trying to tell me you don't have an opinion about the energy crisis? Invent one then, god-damit!" Trudie got her baptism on her first assignment, lining up an interview about the two-hundred-mile fishing limit with Joey Smallwood. While Smallwood was still on the air, Trudie fielded a call from an irate Farley Mowat, demanding a chance to challenge Joey's version of the facts.

Trudie somehow convinced Smallwood to come back so that Mowat and he could do a few rounds of their decades-old feuding on the air.

Tracy Morey was the conscience of the unit, a model of thoughtful judgment and integrity.

Steve Wadhams, the classy and meticulous producer we got from the BBC, has a past that includes soccer commentating for the Malawi Broadcasting Corporation. He has a passion about Africa and its politics, which he tries to specialize in: yet he came up with the best UFO story of them all – Christoff Friedrich and his Nazis under the polar cap.

Edward Trapunski found Mrs. Solzhenitsyn, discovered the House of Dominance, and caused the IRA alert at Heathrow. Edward had a habit of banging his temples with his fists whenever he found a winner for the program, which got to be so regular an occurrence that he finally had to leave us to avoid permanent concussion.

Danny Tobias has two sides to his personality — charming and very charming. It was Danny who knew that Patty Hearst was a good story, who coped with Hayakawa, who found Walter "The Great" Cornelius, and who made sure that Canada got the beaver for its national symbol.

Peter Abrahams fought for Viewpoint, Lloyd Tataryn fought against arsenic and asbestos, and Bill Cobban fought with me about Uri Geller.

Nicole Sakellaropoulo was not only a brilliant producer but also a neat one. When Nicole edited tape, she collected what she couldn't use on an "out" reel, instead of leaving litter on the floor. It seemed a wonderful housekeeping invention, until the night she accidentally played her reject reel to the country. Luckily, the interview was on the Middle East, which, even in the most coherent of discussions, remains a jumble.

In the original *As It Happens* unit were Bill Rockett, Kim Richards, Volkmar Richter, D'Arcy Martin, and Pat Davies. My co-host then was Harry Brown, who's now harnessed his bounce and dedication to his own show.

Sue Helwig, Judy Stoffman, Ian Wakefield, Kelly Crichton, and Barbara Uteck have worked for us from time to time. Our current staff includes Alison Gordon, Alan

Mendelsohn, Dave Hawkins, Anne Howard, and George Jamieson. Patty Habib runs the place and keeps things bubbly. She also knows where everything is, which is lucky for me or there wouldn't have been a book. Helen Knight adroitly fields the calls, complaints, and mail, as have the valiant Helen Krisman and Barbara Colebeck. Technician Ron Grant keeps us airborne, as did Don Logan, Ron Minhinnett, Hedley Jones, and Ashley Russell before him.

Courtly Colin MacLeod, for whom the word subtle was probably invented, was born to manage us and to keep us out of trouble. And splendid Bob Campbell has been chosen to keep it happening and will, I predict, take us on to still greater things.

Finally, my thanks to the CBC, whose air I occupy and whose executives make me feel very appreciated; to Anna Porter, who insisted that this was a book and never wavered; and to Denise Avery, who helped me make it one.

Barbara Frum
July, 1976

About the author

Every weekday night Barbara Frum
conducts the blunt and controversial,
funny and far-out interviews that have
made CBC's *As It Happens* a national
radio favourite. An accomplished journalist, as well as a popular radio and
television personality, she has won two
ACTRA awards, the National Press Club
Journalist of the Year Award, and a
1971 Media Club of Canada Award.
She lives in Toronto with her husband
and three children.